DATE DUE			

B
MAD
2018

32900000049455
Gnojewski, Carol.

Madonna : fighting
for self-expression

**KAMEHAMEHA SCHOOLS KAPALAMA
MIDKIFF LEARNING CENTER**

MADONNA
Fighting for Self-Expression

MADONNA

Fighting for Self-Expression

Enslow Publishing
101 W. 23rd Street
Suite 240
New York, NY 10011
USA

enslow.com

Carol Gnojewski

Published in 2018 by Enslow Publishing, LLC.
101 W. 23rd Street, Suite 240, New York, NY 10011

Library of Congress Cataloging-in-Publication Data

Names: Gnojewski, Carol, author.
Title: Madonna : fighting for self-expression / by Carol Gnojewski.
Description: New York : Enslow Publishing, [2018] | Series: Rebels with a cause |
Includes bibliographical references and index. | Audience: Grades 7–12.
Identifiers: LCCN 2017029955 | ISBN 9780766092556 (library bound)
| ISBN 9780766095526 (paperback)
Subjects: LCSH: Madonna, 1958—Juvenile literature. | Rock musicians—United
States—Biography—Juvenile literature. | Motion picture actors and actresses—
United States—Biography—Juvenile literature.
Classification: LCC ML3930.M26 G65 2018 | DDC 782.42166092 [B] —dc23
LC record available at https://lccn.loc.gov/2017029955

Printed in China

To Our Readers: We have done our best to make sure all website addresses in this
book were active and appropriate when we went to press. However, the author
and the publisher have no control over and assume no liability for the material
available on those websites or on any websites they may link to. Any comments or
suggestions can be sent by email to customerservice@enslow.com.

Portions of this book originally appeared in *Madonna: "Express Yourself"* by Carol
Gnojewski.

CONTENTS

TRODUCTION

After a brief introduction by comedian Amy Schumer, who opened for Madonna's Rebel Heart tour a year earlier, international pop icon Madonna energized protestors who stretched for miles on the streets of our nation's capital when she took to the stage as a surprise guest at the Women's March on Washington on January 21, 2017. In solidarity with more than five million sign-waving, pink-hatted attendees in sister marches around the world supporting women's issues and civil rights, Madonna sported a knitted, cat-eared hat and a matching black T-shirt that defined feminism as "the radical notion that women are people." True to form, she expressed her outrage at the misogynistic rhetoric and xenophobic policies of the newly inaugurated forty-fifth president.

Earlier that month, she'd compared the election to a "horror show." "I wake up and I go, 'Wait a second. Donald Trump is the president. It's not a bad dream. It really happened.' It's like being stuck in a nightmare."[1] Her

On January 21, 2017, Madonna spoke out for women's rights—and against President Donald Trump—at the Women's March on Washington.

rousing, uncensored speech at the Women's March began with an invitation to wake up and shake up the world. She called for a revolution of love to counteract "this new age of tyranny where not just women are in danger but all marginalized people."[2]

The profanity she aimed at detractors was a point of contention with Trump supporters as was her admission of revenge fantasies. "Yes, I'm angry," she said. "Yes, I have thought an awful lot of blowing up the White House, but I know that this won't change anything. We cannot fall into despair."[3]

Her remarks unleashed criticism and calls by conservatives to investigate her perceived threats. President Trump admonished her as a disgrace to the country. "Honestly, she's disgusting," Trump told Fox News. "I think she hurt herself badly. I think she hurt that whole cause."[4]

Madonna was quick to debunk claims she'd advocated for violence. "I spoke in metaphor," she explained, "and I shared two ways of looking at things—one was to be hopeful, and one was to feel anger. I know that acting out of anger doesn't solve anything. The only way to change things for the better is to do it with love."[5]

Speaking out for positive change in the face of conflicting ideologies, and urging others to do the same, has been a consistent theme in over thirty years of Madonna's life in the spotlight. Her Women's March message had particular echoes to the "Get Stupid" medley in her Sticky & Sweet Tour during the 2008 election. As clocks ticked, and images of poverty and corruption were projected on the screen, Madonna sang, "Get up. It's time. Your life, your world."[6] She presented a choice between the misdeeds of dictators and fear-mongers and the hopeful resistance of Gandhi, Martin Luther King Jr., and Mother Theresa.

The political outcome in 2008 resonated more with Madonna's inclusive values. Barack Obama was declared the winner of the forty-fourth presidential race right before a tour performance. An elated Madonna, nearly in tears, exclaimed the following to her giddy cast and crew members in their backstage, preshow huddle:

"Everybody wants change in the world and everybody wants unity. America has slowly degraded itself with all of its greed and consumption and bad leadership and sociopathic behavior. I feel like there's finally light at the end of the tunnel and a chance for us all to come together as one."[7]

Bringing people together to celebrate liberation, equality and diversity is an essential aspect of Madonna's worldview and of her enduring popularity. In another pep talk to the multiracial and gendered cast of her Sticky & Sweet tour, she made these priorities known. "Everybody in here is capable of magic. Everybody in here is capable of changing people's lives, lifting people's spirits, making people think, pushing people's buttons, getting people to believe in their dreams." In Madonna's mind, "That's what art is all about."[8]

What It Feels Like for a Girl

Ironically, the alt-right conservative agenda that Madonna railed against at the Women's March bore a striking resemblance to the period of tax cuts and deregulation ushered in by Republican President Ronald Reagan, which may have enabled Madonna's rapid rise to fame in the early 1980s. Historians referred to the eighties as the "go-go" decade due to the obsession with personal wealth that it fostered, accompanied by an increase in production and consumer spending.

Television was then the dominant medium and video recording technology was in its infancy. In September 1984, pioneer music-video network MTV held their first annual Video Music Awards (VMAs). Hosted by Bette Midler, it was the first awards show to honor the achievements of the innovative artists who helped to shape the fledgling music-video format since the network's emergence three years earlier.

Award-winners that evening included Michael Jackson, Cyndi Lauper, the Eurythmics, Herbie Hancock, and ZZ Top. But the highlight of the show was the now-classic performance of a young, upcoming vocalist named Madonna, previewing her sophomore album with a live rendition of the chart-topping "Like a Virgin."

Madonna made history when she performed her single "Like a Virgin" live at the 1984 MTV Video Music Awards at New York's Radio City Music Hall.

Strands of white lights formed twinkling arches above a gigantic three-tiered wedding cake with a life-size bride and groom as the cake topper. As the music began, the bride stepped forward and lifted her veil. Madonna emerged, clad in white lace gloves that hugged her muscular arms, and a sexy bridal dress with a white, lace bustier top. A leather belt that read "Boy Toy" held up a tulle skirt sprinkled with polka dot hearts.

Madonna descended the white staircase built into the cake, crucifix necklaces swinging. She sweetly sang about past relationships and finding true love. As the music quickened, she removed the veil and tossed it to the floor. Sauntering downstage, she taunted and teased the bewildered yet cheering audience. "Never before," one reporter stated, "has a wedding dress looked more like a

A REAL "THRILLER"

In 1984, superstar Michael Jackson won the Viewer's Choice Award for "Thriller," the first long-form video shown on MTV. The fourteen-minute video told the story of a couple whose date takes a surreal turn when they cut through a graveyard on their way home from a horror movie. Jackson, the first major black artist to appear on MTV, revolutionized the concept of the music video with storytelling and lavishly choreographed dance sequences. Previously, record companies conceived these videos as low-budget promotional items.

sleazy go-go outfit."[2] Shattering the myth of the chaste, virginal bride, Madonna touched herself and rolled around the stage bumping and grinding. Her new love, she sang, made her feel "shiny and new."

Fast-forward to the summer of 2003. The twentieth annual Video Music Awards opens with a bridal backdrop complete with a flowered archway and a giant wedding cake. Two flower girls walk across the stage strewing petals on the floor. Madonna fans recognize them as six-year-old Lourdes, Madonna's eldest daughter, and her friend, Honour.

A bride bursts out of the wedding cake. She lifts her veil to reveal—not Madonna—but pop sensation Britney Spears. Soon her pop rival, Christina Aguilera, also

Nearly twenty years after her MTV VMA debut, Madonna was back to stir up more controversy, this time with the help of fellow singers Britney Spears (*left*) and Christina Aguilera (*right*), with whom she shared scandalous lip-locks during the 2003 awards show.

dressed as a bride, joins her in a joint rendition of "Like a Virgin." The homage continues as the bridal duo roll and writhe across the dance floor.

At the end of the song, Madonna materializes from the cake. This time, she is dressed as a bridegroom with top hat and tails. She dominates the stage, performing her single "Hollywood," from the *American Life* album. The brides function as her backup singers. Throughout the song, Madonna clutches Britney's waist and strokes her face. Provocatively, she removes the garter from Christina's thigh and throws it into the audience. Before

BOY TOY

Boy Toy was Madonna's graffiti tag name.[1] Madonna befriended graffiti artists Keith Haring and Jean-Michel Basquiat when all three were starting out in NYC. Both died tragically young—Basquiat from a drug overdose and Haring from AIDS. Madonna later used Haring's bright, cartoonish designs as the backdrop for the playful "Into the Groove" segment of her Sticky & Sweet Tour, in which she and her dancers jumped rope in tandem. She further immortalized their friendship in the song "Graffiti Heart" from the *Rebel Heart* album. Boy Toy became the name of her copyright company and that of a clothing collection featuring Madonna-inspired fashions. To her tongue-in-cheek sensibility, the moniker meant, "I toy with boys."

the conclusion of the number, Madonna manages to french kiss both brides.

These lipstick kisses caused nearly as much controversy as Madonna's first, attention-grabbing VMA appearance. Photos of Madonna and Spears locking lips appeared worldwide in tabloids and newspapers. An internet poll circulated entitled "The Kiss Heard 'Round the World." It asked for "Your take on the Big Kiss."[3]

The reaction of many was unsurprisingly negative. Some condemned Madonna and her younger protégées for female lechery while others singled out Madonna as ringleader, chastising her for exposing her daughter to "immoral" and "pornographic" behavior. Progressive websites at the time read more into the performance. They viewed the skit as embracing lesbian sexuality and as a possible endorsement of gay marriage.[4]

Shortly after the awards, Spears insisted that the kiss was a harmless publicity stunt planned for ahead of time. "I didn't know it was going to be that long and everything," said Spears, who benefited from the kiss by shedding her squeaky-clean Mouseketeer image.[5] Years later, Madonna publicly explained the meaning of the kiss to Lourdes. "I am the mommy pop star and she [Spears] is the baby pop star. And I am kissing her to pass my energy onto her."[6]

A League of Her Own

Madonna's live appearance in the 1984 MTV Video Music Awards was the first shocking moment in a career seemingly built on controversy. From her pointy bras to her public love life to her tell-all documentaries and banned videos, Madonna has consistently "caused a commotion," parodying sexual stereotypes, such as the gold-digging blonde, the pregnant teen, and the all-American cowgirl.

She embodies the conception of celebrity as an all-purpose entertainment package. Journalist Jennifer Egan theorizes that "[her] contribution has been to usher in the phenomenon of star as multimedia impresario. She's a creator of extravaganza, and she does this using imagery, sound, her voice, her body and anything else she can scare up."[7] Madonna belongs, Egan believes, in a classification of stars "defined less by any single talent or pursuit than by an array of projects and endeavors whose combined impact expands their personae exponentially."[8]

Madonna perceives creativity as inherently selfish. "What I did, I did for myself, to free myself. I never really planned to be an idol for millions of women all over the planet."[9] She is drawn to projects that strike a chord with her on many levels, and that she believes will help her evolve as an artist. "What am I going to learn from it? Is it going to challenge me? Is it going to take me to another place?" are some of the questions she asks herself.[10]

Yet her legacy has given direction to many young pop stars. Rapper Nicki Minaj, who has appeared in Madonna videos and live shows, has remarked, "When I think of greatness and what a legend is, I always think of Madonna."[11] In *Rolling Stone* magazine, Britney Spears acknowledged, "I would definitely not be here, doing what I'm doing, if it wasn't for Madonna. I remember being eight or nine years old, running around my living room singing and dancing and wanting so much to be like her. As part of the generation that's coming up, you look at Madonna and you don't want to let her down."[12]

2

Mother and Father

During her 1984 appearance on the live dance show *American Bandstand*, host Dick Clark asked Madonna what she planned to do when she grew up. Madonna's brash reply was "Mmmm, to rule the world."[1] Decades later, with countless albums, world tours, films, and books to her credit, Madonna seems to have achieved this goal. Often referred to as the Queen of Pop, the Guinness Book of World Records cites Madonna as the most successful female recording artist of all time.

Yet Madonna's journey toward international stardom represents a long, calculated effort. Her drive for achievement and recognition began in childhood. She entered the world on August 16, 1958, as Madonna Louise Ciccone (chuh-KONE-ee), the eldest daughter of Silvio (Tony) Ciccone and Madonna Fortin. Absorbing and eventually rejecting her parents' conservative, Midwestern values helped to shape her independent spirit.

The youngest of six children in a first-generation Italian-American family, Tony was a devout Catholic with a strong work ethic. He became the first in his family to attend college and obtained a job as an engineer for the Chrysler Corporation. A former Air Force Reservist, in 1955 he married Madonna Fortin, the sister of military buddy Dale Fortin, whom he'd met at Dale's wedding.

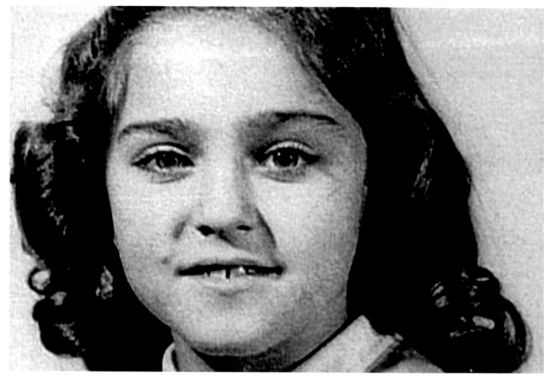

Madonna, shown here in a school photo at age nine, grew up in the small town of Pontiac, Michigan. She was one of six children in a large Italian Catholic family.

Settling in the small town of Pontiac, Michigan, the young couple had six children together: Anthony, Martin, Madonna, Christopher, Paula, and Melanie.

Madonna's mother and namesake was an intelligent, deeply religious woman with interests in dance, classical music, and medicine. Unlike her husband, she hailed from an established, middle-class family with an impressive pioneer pedigree. Her French-Canadian ancestors were noted for such resoluteness and tenacity that, according to maternal relative Claire Narbonne-Fortin, "Nothing Madonna Junior does ever surprises us."[2]

Madonna's grandmother Elsie Fortin believed their marriage was a happy one. "My son-in-law was proud of the way my daughter looked and kept the house," she has stated. "They were always very warm and loving in front of the children."[3] Madonna's earliest memories corroborate this nurturing domestic portrait. In interviews she often refers to her mother as a playful and patient person, dancing and singing with her children to the radio and always picking up after everyone.

Familial bliss, however, was relatively short lived. In 1962, six months after the birth of her daughter Melanie, Madonna's mother was diagnosed with breast cancer. After a gradual decline and extensive hospitalization, she succumbed to cancer one year later at the age of thirty. Madonna was five years old at the time of her mother's death. She attributes this event, and the realization of her own mortality, to the end of her childhood and the beginning of her drive to make a creative impact on

THE GOOD LIFE

Lyrics from the song "Easy Ride," on Madonna's *American Life* album, seem to reflect her father's self-reliant attitude, born out of the prosperous 1950s, when the middle class thrived. They speak of wanting the "good life," the realization of the American Dream, but without a sense of entitlement. The main character pulls himself up by his bootstraps, rejecting the notion of an easy ride. The song suggests that success and self-dignity belong to those willing to sacrifice the "blood and sweat" of hard work and perseverance to achieve goals.

the world. Madonna explained, "I've got to push myself so hard because I have demons. I won't live forever and when I die I don't want people to forget I existed."[4]

The trauma of losing her mother at an early age has directly informed Madonna's work. *Truth or Dare*, the 1991 documentary of her Blond Ambition tour, featured a scene in which she and her younger brother Christopher visit the cemetery where their mother is buried. Madonna proceeds to lie down on top of the grave, while struggling to articulate her sense of loss. In a 1998 review of her *Ray of Light* album, a reporter wrote, "The third song in this personal trilogy is "Mer Girl," in which Madonna seems to be reconciling the death of her mother through the birth of her daughter [Lourdes]. 'I ran from my mother who haunts me/ from my daughter that never sleeps/ I ran and I ran, I'm still running away,' she sings."[5]

Lyrics from the autobiographical song "Mother and Father" further reflect upon her mother's death. In this song, Madonna emphasizes the childhood perspective with repetitive, sing-song rhymes, reminiscent of school yard chants. As a young girl of five, she's aware of a lost connection. She copes with her mother's death through the self-comfort of crying, but doesn't understand why her mother isn't there to pacify her.

After her mother's death, Madonna's immediate reaction was to withdraw into herself and her family, acting maternally toward her younger siblings and possessive of her father's attention. Housekeepers and babysitters were hired to supervise them while he worked. In 1966, three years after his wife's death, Tony Ciccone married Joan Gustafson. At twenty-three, Joan was twelve years his junior. She had been their housekeeper for six months.

Madonna and her father, Tony Ciccone, appeared together during a taping of Arsenio Hall's talk show in 1992. As a teenager, Madonna and her father had a very strained relationship.

When asked to describe herself as an adolescent, Madonna has replied, "I see a very lonely girl who was searching for something, looking for a mother figure."[6] Yet she's professed she was unwilling to allow her stepmother to fulfill that role for her. "My father made us all call her Mom," she said, but "I couldn't, I wouldn't say it."[7]

Madonna missed her real mother and resented her stepmother's intrusion. Joan Gustafson ran a strict, clean, and orderly home and expected her new family to pitch in with the housework. Madonna told *Time* magazine, "I was the oldest girl. I feel like all my adolescence was spent taking care of babies and changing diapers and baby-sitting. I have to say I resented it, because when all my friends were out playing, I had all these adult responsibilities. I think that's when I really thought about how I wanted to do something else and get away from all that. I really saw myself as the quintessential Cinderella."[8]

Papa Don't Preach

Following the arrival of two new siblings, Jennifer and Mario, the now ten-member Ciccone family moved to a red brick, Colonial-style home in Rochester, Michigan, a suburb of Detroit. This upscale, all-white neighborhood proved a repressive environment for the artistic souls of Madonna and her younger brother, Christopher. He summarizes their reaction to Midwestern suburbia as follows: "Most of our aesthetic is rebellion against what we grew up with—the 70s version of Colonial, the spindle-back chairs, the fake spinning wheel in the corner, the wooden icebox that held records."[9]

The change of surroundings resulting from their move coincided with the emotional and physiological changes of puberty for Madonna. She remembers being punished for her outspokenness, especially when questioning what she regarded as the "injustices of her religious upbringing." Rules enforced by her father and other authority figures simply didn't make sense to her budding consciousness. She explained her motivation to assert her individuality

ALL IN THE FAMILY

Christopher, a multitalented artist, has worked closely with his sister in many capacities. He accompanied her on her worldwide tours until 2003. Other family members she has employed include her half-brother Mario, who worked at Madonna's record company, Maverick; her daughter Lourdes, who worked in the wardrobe department during the MDNA tour and with whom she launched the teen fashion brand Material Girl in 2010; and her son Rocco Ritchie, who appeared in her MDNA and Rebel Heart tours.

amidst the Catholic discipline as follows: "When you go to Catholic school, you have to wear uniforms, and everything is decided for you. Since you have no choice but to wear your uniform, you go out of your way to do things that are different in order to stand out."[10]

Her reputation as a wild child was fueled by a tendency toward exhibitionism. In the finale of a junior high talent show, she flashed the audience. After performing to the song "Secret Agent Man," she revealed that all she wore under her oversized trench coat was a dance leotard. Her dance routines outraged parents and teachers despite the ovations she received from fellow classmates. Madonna, who attended Catholic schools until high school, later defended her schoolgirl provocation, insisting "the talent show was my one night a year to show them who I really was and what I could really be, and I just wanted to do totally outrageous stuff."[11]

These audacious pubescent shenanigans prefigure her later video-oriented career. Each night of her first tour, aptly named the Virgin Tour, ended with a nod to the effects of her stage presence on parental authority. When the concert played hometown Detroit, she convinced her father to come out onstage and escort her off. At other engagements, a taped voice-over of a stern male voice ordered her offstage, to which she coyly replied, "Daddy, do I hafta?"[12]

3

You Can Dance, for Inspiration

As Madonna got older, her home life became increasingly competitive. She vied for her father's attention, and felt like an outsider at home. Chores and schoolwork dominated her life. Her brothers reacted to this strict, goal-oriented upbringing by escaping into psychedelic music and drugs. Madonna's desire for attention led her on a path toward artistic experimentation. "I wasn't rebellious in a conventional way," she has explained about her high school years. "I cared about being good at something. I studied hard and got good grades."[1]

No one pushed Madonna harder than herself. She juggled an active social life with a busy after-school routine. She took classes in piano and jazz dance, and she participated in cheerleading, French club, and choir. She also helped to found the Rochester Adams High School Thespian Society. "Every time there was a talent show or a musical at school, I was always in it," she said.[2]

Madonna's high school drama teacher, Beverly Gibson, believed her to be a popular student with great charisma and a strong stage presence. However, Madonna professed that she struggled to fit in with her peers until she found her niche in ballet. "When I was in the tenth grade I knew a girl who was a serious ballet dancer. She looked smarter than your average girl but in an interesting, offbeat

Madonna's senior photo from Adams High School, in Rochester, Michigan, in 1976. After graduation, Madonna attended the University of Michigan but dropped out in 1978 to move to New York and pursue a career in dance.

way. So I attached myself to her and she brought me to a ballet class, and that's where I met Christopher Flynn, who saved me from my high school turmoil."[3]

Some Madonna devotees tout Christopher Flynn as "arguably the first Madonna-positive person."[4] Lyrics from "In This Life" on Madonna's *Erotica* album attempt to explain his lasting influence on her. Madonna refers to Flynn as a loving father figure who taught her to respect herself. She also communicates the belief that people should not be judged by their sexual orientation.

Ballet quickly became a lifestyle for Madonna. The self-discipline necessary for growth as a dancer transformed her personality from a wise-cracking show-off to an introspective, somewhat aloof nonconformist. Becoming more comfortable with her body through dance may have helped her to develop confidence and ease with herself and her own sense of style. She cut her hair short and wore clothes that clashed, such as overalls and bold-printed shirts with combat boots. Remarking on her high school appearance, friend Lisa Gaggino remembers, "She wasn't afraid to be different, and at that age it's hard to be different without worrying what other people think of you."[6] Madonna later explained her style, "Where is it written that in order to be a better dancer you have to wear a black leotard and pink tights and have your hair in a bun?"[7]

Dance was a gateway for discovery in other arts in which she has maintained a lifelong interest. Impressed with Madonna's talent and ambition, Flynn took it upon himself to become her mentor, exposing her to Detroit's museums, operas, concerts, art galleries, and fashion shows. One of Flynn's friends explains that Chris "knew without ever meeting her family that Madonna lacked any cultural or intellectual background and yet he was certain

DANCING GIRL

Flynn ran the Rochester School of Ballet. He had studied under Vladimir Dokoudovsky, a student of George Balanchine, who approached dance as theater.[5] During his dance career, Flynn performed in the prestigious Joffrey Ballet Company. His was a professional dance studio, and most of his pupils had been trained in ballet from an early age. Although Madonna had taken a variety of dance classes, she came to him a virtual novice. She had to work very hard to match the abilities of the group.

that all she needed was someone to take her under his wing."[8] At home she read teen magazines like *Seventeen* and listened to popular bands such as the Monkees and the Jackson Five. With Flynn, her tastes broadened to include classical music, Pre-Raphaelite painters, and poets such as Sylvia Plath and Anne Sexton. "My sister and I used to read all of her [Anne Sexton's] poems when we were in high school because she looked like our mother," Madonna said. "She talks about death a lot and breast cancer and mothers, all these death images that we were obsessed with."[9]

Flynn also was the first person to introduce Madonna to homosexuality. "I didn't understand the concept of gay at that time," she's since revealed. "All I knew was that my ballet teacher was different from everybody else. He had a certain theatricality about him. He made you proud of yourself; just the way he came up to me and put my face in his hand and said, 'You are beautiful.' I fell in love with him and the way he treated me."[10]

Madonna felt accepted around Flynn and his friends. When she accompanied Flynn to gay discotheques she felt free to cut loose and dance uninhibitedly. Regarding her teenage exploration of gay subculture, Madonna has said, "In school and in my neighborhood and everything, I felt like such a misfit. And suddenly when I went to the gay club, I didn't feel that way anymore. I just felt at home. I had a whole new sense of myself."[11]

It is not surprising that her entrée into gay culture was so enlightening. When Madonna's brother Christopher began taking ballet lessons, Flynn was quick to point out to Madonna that Christopher was gay. Flynn was likewise a confidante for her own bisexual experimentation with Kathy, the serious ballet student who first introduced

Madonna got her start as a dancer, studying ballet and popular dance by day and going to clubs at night to blow off steam and try out new moves.

her to Flynn's ballet class. Though not an exclusive relationship, their affair supposedly lasted through high school and into their early twenties.[12]

You'll See

Christopher Flynn paved the way for Madonna to leave Rochester Hills to pursue her dance dreams. In 1976, he accepted a visiting professorship in the dance program at University of Michigan, Ann Arbor. He convinced Madonna to graduate early from high school and apply for a scholarship through the Michigan Music Department where she could continue to study under him. His influence must have helped her to win a full four-year dance scholarship to this institution. However, Madonna's own intelligence and talent proved equally instrumental in propelling her forward. Academically, she ranked high in her class, and her teachers wrote glowing recommendations to the scholarship committee, praising her motivation and creativity.

> **"If I can't be daring in my work or the way I live my life, then I don't really see the point of being on this planet." — Madonna**

Madonna has admitted that her father would have "freaked out" if he had known of the intensity of her relationship with Flynn and of their frequent forays to gay nightclubs. Though pleased by her scholarship, the practical Tony held reservations about dance as a career. Madonna said about her father, "He's a sensible guy, and what's dancing to him? He can't imagine that you can make a living from it or think of it as an accomplishment."[13] From this point onward, Madonna carefully constructed her own support network.

Once at Michigan, Madonna committed herself to a demanding dance schedule. In 1977, she won a scholarship for a summer apprenticeship in a student company at the Alvin Ailey American Dance Theatre in New York. At that time, Ailey's company had its headquarters in the American Dance Center on East Fifty-Ninth Street. They shared a building with the dance company of Pearl Lang, formerly a soloist for the legendary Martha Graham. Lang and her dancers occupied the ground floor while Ailey's group rehearsed in the upper floors.

When Madonna returned to Michigan her sophomore year, Lang surfaced as an artist-in-residence. Madonna danced in a recital of a new work Lang created for the university. By this time, Madonna was impatient to go to NYC and train with a professional dance company. Flynn encouraged her in this goal. The prevailing myth, a myth Madonna helped to perpetuate in her 1983 interview in *Star Hits* magazine shortly after her first album debut, professes that Madonna arrived in NYC in the summer of 1978 with only thirty-five dollars and a lot of ambition.[16]

ALVIN AILEY

Founded in 1958 by African-American dancer/choreographer Alvin Ailey, the Ailey Dance Theatre blends classical, jazz, modern, and African-American movement traditions. Ailey's mission was to break color and ethnic barriers by providing a multiracial dance environment. According to Jennifer Dunning's biography, *Alvin Ailey: A Life in Dance*, hundreds of young New Yorkers and would-be dancers from around the country converged on the school.[14] Madonna acknowledges the exhilaration and intimidation of that summer school experience. "Everyone was Hispanic or black," she said, "and everyone wanted to be a star."[15]

It was a gutsy decision to abandon her degree, her scholarship, and supportive friends like Flynn. However, Madonna didn't take this risk unprepared. College friends concur that she worked nights and weekends to amass a substantial nest egg. Madonna didn't spend much time in New York that summer. She headed to Duke University for the American Dance Festival where Pearl Lang, as guest faculty choreographer, awarded Madonna a festival scholarship. At the end of the festival, she approached Lang for a position in her company and Lang consented.

Lang decisively asserts herself as Madonna's primary ballet and modern-dance mentor, subsequent to her university training. She considered Madonna to be a beautiful performer with "the most gorgeous back."[17] This is high praise coming from the premier Martha Graham protégé (in Graham's philosophy, the impulse of all movement stems from a dancer's back).

Lang looked out for Madonna, using her personal connections to find her employment as a coat-check girl to help pay for her expenses. She also invited her to parties at her apartment. Yet the daily routine and Spartan demands of Lang's choreography wore on Madonna. Passions ran high between them. A dancer describes the two squaring off before the company. "It was like watching two tigresses prowling around, sizing each other up." [18]

Madonna felt stifled in the competitive atmosphere of the professional New York dance circuit, where progress within a company is often slow and uncertain. She eventually confronted Lang, announcing that she was going to become a rock singer instead of a dancer. "With all that promise she gave up dancing," said Lang. "The problem with her from the beginning was that she was never willing to see a discipline through to the end."

4

She's a Real Disco Queen

Under Lang's tutelage, Madonna inhabited a sophisticated social circle that included fine art
lovers and New York intellectuals. Meanwhile,
worlds apart from this artistic environment, pop culture
from the mid-1970s through the early 1980s underwent a
disco dance craze.

French singer Patrick Hernandez rocketed to
international stardom with his 1978 disco hit, "Born to
Be Alive." His producers held open auditions in New York
in 1979 for a worldwide tour. They were seeking backup
dancers and singers and Madonna stood out among the
fifteen hundred hopefuls. They decided to bring her to
Paris and groom her as a star. "We saw right away that
she had more punch than the others," Hernandez said.
"Instead of selecting her to dance like an idiot behind me,
we separated her from the other performers. We wanted
to bring her to France so she could record."[1]

Despite her announcement to Lang, Madonna still
identified herself as a dancer. Utilizing Hernandez's
connections, she envisioned becoming a dancer/actress.
Her Parisian patrons, though, intended to develop and
market Madonna as another disco singer. They paid
her expenses, and they arranged for music, singing,
dancing and conversational French lessons. They even

THE DAYS OF DISCO

"Disco" is short for *discotheque*—the French word for nightclub, particularly those that featured recorded music rather than live bands. The music of the late 1960s and early 1970s was dominated by groups that emerged from the folk-rock movement, such as Simon and Garfunkel and show bands like Jefferson Airplane. Disco took its roots from funk and soul music. Its up-tempo, "four to the floor" bass line catered to the intimate sphere of the dance club rather than a massive concert crowd.

commissioned a song for her, entitled "She's a Real Disco Queen."

Madonna grew deeply dissatisfied with the pace of her career as dictated by her managers. She also didn't respond well to the disco music that they wanted her to sing. At the time, she preferred the punk sound of singers such as Debbie Harry of Blondie or Chrissie Hynde of the Pretenders. In retrospect, Hernandez finds her resentment of disco ironic. "Funny," he has said, "when she became a success years later, it was by singing the kinds of pop dance tunes we were trying to get her to record in the first place."[2]

Hernandez believes that his fame motivated Madonna and proved to be a lasting influence. He and his friends succeeded in convincing her that she could become a major recording star. However, she was prepared to take her chances back in the United States. Weeks before leaving for Paris, Madonna encountered the Gilroy brothers. She met Dan Gilroy and his brother Ed at a party thrown by a mutual friend. Dan and Madonna quickly became an item and kept up a long-distance flirtation. When Madonna returned from Europe, she moved in with them.

Twelve years her senior, Dan Gilroy seized the baton from Christopher Flynn as life-changing creative male mentor. For nearly a year, Gilroy supported Madonna and furthered her music education. He encouraged her in her songwriting pursuits and taught her how to play the guitar and drums, which showcased her energy and rhythmic abilities. Madonna continued dancing, but now practiced on drums and guitar just as fervently. An avid diarist, she also began to use material she wrote in her journals as the basis for song lyrics. Her first attempts at songwriting are perceived as an important self-revelation. "I don't know where they came from," she is quoted as saying. "It was like magic. I'd write a song every day. I said: 'Wow, I was meant to do this.'"[3]

Dan, as singer/songwriter, and Ed, as lead guitarist, headed a punk rock garage band named the Breakfast Club. As Madonna's musical talent emerged, she joined the band. Other members included Gary Burke as bassist, and Mike Monahan on drums. Madonna frequently shared vocals with the Gilroys, singing duets and solo numbers. They began to attract the attention of club owners. Madonna was eager to front the band herself and to secure a record deal. The Gilroys, though, refused to accept her lead or to favor her material to the exclusion of theirs. By summer 1980, Madonna quit the band. She explains her decision to end her relationship with them: "They weren't as interested in the commercial end as I was. It never occurred to me to get into this business and not be a huge success."[4]

Along with Burke and drummer Stephen Bray, Madonna formed the band Emmy. It took nearly a year for the band to establish a foothold in the local club scene. Away from the safety and luxury of the Gilroys, Madonna faced tough times. She lived in squalid conditions, sometimes without the means to pay for heat. She accepted cast-off clothing and makeup from friends. Impatience and desperation nearly drove her to return to her family in Michigan.

Madonna received her big break in the spring of 1981 when Emmy performed at the popular nightspot Max's Kansas City. At the time, Adam Alter and Camille Barbone headed Gotham Sound Studios, a recording studio located in the same building where Emmy rehearsed. Madonna managed to persuade Alter to listen to a tape of Emmy songs. He convinced Barbone to scout Madonna during their show. Impressed with Madonna but not with what she described as her "lousy band,"[5] Barbone agreed to manage her as a solo performer. At the same time, the management at Max's, owners of an independent record label, offered Emmy a recording contract.

After years of struggle, Madonna received two attractive contract offers in one night. Madonna chose the option that thrust her alone in the spotlight. Her collaboration with Gotham Sound Studios didn't last long. Madonna and Barbone disagreed about musical direction. She and Alter were primarily interested in rock and roll whereas Madonna began to embrace disco. She walked out on her contract in February 1982. Barbone contends Madonna was stolen away from her. "After networking and generally managing Madonna smack into the middle of mainstream music, the word got out." People began to contact her directly and promise her things I couldn't deliver. I wasn't a member of the good old boy network of managers and labels that work hand and hand," she said.[6]

Where's the Party?

Going to clubs in the early 1980s seemed to be the best way to experience the latest dance music. Madonna carefully observed the dancing she liked best, and she developed her own danceable tunes. She realized that funky dance records were in style on the radio and on the dance floor. Reuniting with Stephen Bray, she recorded a demo tape with four dance tracks, including "Burning Up," "Everybody," and "Ain't No Big Deal." Madonna describes her music as "the kind that helps people to forget about the problems of the world. People go out to dance to get away and forget about their problems like a holiday and that's what the music's about—to get together and forget."[7]

Once again a free agent, but now with contacts and exposure, Madonna did her own legwork to promote her demo, systematically touring night clubs and discos to meet music business professionals. Madonna's ambition led her to the Manhattan nightclub Danceteria. Danceteria was the place to be seen—a celebrity hangout then considered one of the hippest venues in New York. Madonna said, "'I used to go to Danceteria every weekend, trying to meet the DJ or an A&R (artist and repertoire) person to give my tape to. I'd spend all night on the dance floor.[8]

Vito Bruno, a club manager, stated, "Madonna and her friends were the kinds of kids you wanted in your venue.

In 1985, Madonna, already known for her singing and dancing, became a certified triple threat when she starred in the movie *Desperately Seeking Susan*, which became a 1980s cult favorite.

PARTY ALL THE TIME

Madonna was in her element on the dance floor. She created her own style; layered thrift store finds with lots of accessories—leggings, miniskirts or baggy pants tied with ribbons, cropped denim jackets, mesh tank tops, lingerie used as outerwear, and fingerless gloves. Her dance moves were suggestive and aggressive, with pelvic grinds that showed off her bare midriff, and sexy twirls punctuated by flirty head tosses. Madonna describes the attitude she exemplified: "American clubs [were] perfect but temporary democracies of desire, an ideal world where racial, sexual and social divisions were dissolved in the communal abandon of the dance floor. The mass euphoria and emotional solidarity I experienced while dancing at downtown clubs seemed like a possible model for a future society."[10]

She was a standout—trendy and eye-catching. They got into the VIP rooms before they were VIP's."[9]

Eventually, her persistence paid off. At Danceteria, she met DJ Mark Kamins, an A&R scout for Island Records, which represented pop acts such as U2. Kamins recalls the day he first gave her songs a spin. "Madonna was a regular at the Danceteria. She had great style and had to be the center of attraction. One day she gave me a demo—it worked. I knew the people at Sire Records. I played them the demo and they gave me a single deal. I produced "Everybody" and it went to #1 in the dance charts. The rest is history."[11]

5
Star Light, Star Bright

S ire's strategy mirrored what Madonna had been doing all along—promoting her singing and dancing
abilities in nightclubs. They produced a string of
one-song albums that received club exposure, then radio
airtime. Following the success of "Everybody," they released "Burning Up," "Lucky Star," and "Holiday" in 1983.
These songs were compiled on her first album, *Madonna*.

John "Jellybean" Benitez, who produced "Holiday,"
was resident DJ of the Fun House, a Manhattan club
frequented by rap and hip-hop artists such as LL Cool
J and Lisa Lisa. Madonna made frequent stops at the
Fun House, and she began a tempestuous two-year
relationship with him. He and Madonna seemed to be
truly in love, and they soon became engaged. They made
a great team and helped each other through the trauma of
budding celebrity. A shrewd and ambitious businessman,
Benitez showed Madonna how to manipulate the media
and exploit her position in the industry.

Madonna personally controlled her career. Each Friday
she joined Sire promoter Bobby Shaw and club DJs for
business meetings in his office. She also secured a high-
powered manager, Freddy DeMann, who had worked for
Michael Jackson. Her association with DeMann lasted
several decades. DeMann immediately sought to market

During her first national tour in 1985, Madonna traveled across the country, performing for thousands of new fans. Here she's shown singing for Seattle fans.

Madonna to a mass audience through the fledgling medium of music videos.

Academic Pamela Robertson touts music videos as representing "the post-modern explosion of technologies, acceleration of images and information, and mass-media access."[1] Robertson views Madonna as "the ultimate postmodern video star," comfortable with image, representation, and artifice as features of music production. Music videos allowed her to merge her dance training with her musical abilities. She already had two music videos under her belt, "Everybody" and "Burning

A STORIED CAREER

"Borderline" has a straightforward story line. A streetwise Madonna, discovered by a fashion photographer while break dancing, leaves her friends and Latino boyfriend behind. Eventually, however, Madonna becomes bored and is kicked out of the photographer's studio. She returns to her colorful street life to win back her boyfriend. Her manager, DeMann, correctly believed that pop songs such as "Borderline," supported by professional videos, would garner mainstream appeal. Madonna has made at least sixty-nine music videos and has won twenty MTV Video Music Awards.

Up," before making a splash in the pop classic "Borderline," directed by Mary Lambert.

For Madonna, the transition from live musical performance to film seemed natural. This wasn't the case for established musicians who believed their music was more important than imagery. At a New Music Seminar panel held in New York in 1984, Madonna defends the music video format. "I'm sorry," she said, "but kids today worship the television, so I think it's a great way to reach them."[2] When John Oates of Hall and Oates countered that he resented the necessity of being an actor as well as a musician in videos, Madonna quipped, "Yeah but, but listen. When you perform on-stage you're acting. I mean that's the performance. If someone puts a camera on you what's the difference?"[3]

Later that year Madonna attempted to explain her ease in front of the camera in the article "Madonna Goes All the Way" for *Rolling Stone* magazine. Writer Christopher Connelly asks the question: How did she manage to put across such seething sexuality where so many [recording artists] have tried and failed? Madonna replies, "I think that has to do with them not being in touch with that part of themselves to begin with. I've been in touch with that aspect of my personality since I was five."[4]

Into the Groove

To boost profit margins on her first album, Sire delayed the release of her next album, *Like a Virgin*, until November 1984. For *Like a Virgin*, which she playfully dedicated to the virgins of the world, Madonna had her pick of producers. She decided upon Nile Rodgers, who had successfully engineered records for Diana Ross and David Bowie. "I chose to work with Nile Rodgers," she told MTV News, "because I think that he's a genius and I wanted to work with a genius."[5]

A skilled musician, Rodgers may also have been chosen for his expertise in arranging songs. Madonna's musical ear was primarily instinctual. She had never received significant music training and did not know music terminology. For most of the songs on the album, she collaborated with Stephen Bray. Bray describes their songwriting process, "I've always kind of made the rib cage and the skeleton [music] of the song already—she's there for the last things like the eyebrows and the haircut [lyrics]. She writes in a stream of mood really."[6]

Madonna is shown here performing in Madrid in 1990. She has always been known for her wild, trend-setting fashions, and in the 1990s, her cone-shaped bra became a signature piece of clothing.

Madonna later corroborated her habit of getting into a certain mood and writing from it. In 1989, she admitted that in her first albums she was primarily interested in coming across as "entertaining and charming and frivolous and sweet."[7] At the time of that interview, her sixth album, *Like a Prayer*, had just been released. Unlike her other albums, she recorded *Like a Prayer* in the studio with live musicians, rather than overdubbing the vocals on top of the finished music. Although her approach to recording her music had evolved, Madonna's method of developing songs had not changed since her first releases. It remains a group effort.

"Sometimes the music is sort of there, already written by either Pat Leonard [an arranger/producer] or Stephen Bray. They give it to me and it inspires or insinuates a lyric or feeling. Then I write out the words in a free form, and we change the music to fit the form. Other times I'll start out with lyrics, or I'll have written a poem and I'll want to put that to music. Then I end up changing the words a little bit to make them more musical."[8]

The success of her first albums and videos opened up other opportunities for her. In 1983, DeMann arranged for her involvement in the movie *Vision Quest*, in which she has a cameo as a night club singer. This resulted in the videos "Crazy for You" and "Gambler." Film exposure led to the title role in the upbeat screwball comedy *Desperately Seeking Susan*, which was set in NYC.

Taking advantage of Madonna's rising popularity, director Susan Seidelman filmed an extensive nightclub sequence in Madonna's old haunt the Danceteria, showcasing her song "Into the Groove," which became a successful follow-up single. Many critics therefore hailed *Desperately Seeking Susan* as "Madonna's Movie."

DESPERATELY SEEKING SUSAN

Although the film was originally intended to be a star vehicle for actress Rosanna Arquette, director Susan Seidelman expanded Madonna's role in *Desperately Seeking Susan* on the strength of her unforgettable characterization of the street-wise Susan. The plot centers on a bored housewife, Roberta [Arquette], who becomes obsessed with an adventurer named Susan [Madonna] who she encounters in the personal ads. After adopting Susan's manner of dress, Roberta has an accident and gets amnesia. She then believes she's Susan, and the mistaken identity leads to mayhem.

Madonna's finesse in this role came as no surprise to her manager Freddy DeMann. He believed the part was made for her. Though she later appeared in over a dozen movies, she was destined to "desperately seek" another film role that suited her abilities for over a decade. Arguably, playing herself in her documentary *Truth or Dare*, and her portrayal of the cartoon gangster's moll Breathless Mahoney in the film *Dick Tracy*, are exceptions. But not until her characterization of Eva Perón in the 1996 movie musical *Evita* would Madonna again receive rave reviews for her feature film work.

Why's It So Hard

By 1985, Madonna was an international celebrity. The critical and commercial success of her albums, videos, and films prompted *Time* magazine to feature her on its cover. Fame had its downside. Ironically, for a take-charge "Material Girl," juggling her financial rewards seemed stressful. In her video for this number one single, Madonna wittily parodies the gold-digging attributes of sex symbol Marilyn Monroe. Wearing a dress copied from the Marilyn Monroe hit film *Gentlemen Prefer Blondes*, in which Monroe announces that diamonds are a girl's best friend, Madonna's video persona longs for men with cold, hard cash.

Feminist theorists such as Sonya Andermahr embraced Madonna's self-reliance, claiming that "Madonna calls her own shots … [S]he exercises more power and control over the production, marketing and financial value of her image than any female icon before her."[1] Yet, an interview with *MTV News* around this time captures her angst. "Well now that I am successful I have a million more things to worry about. Before I was just basically interested in my survival."[2]

Her love life also seems to have been strained. Early in the year she broke off her engagement with Jellybean Benitez, who was willing to start a family with her. In

From 1985 to 1989, Madonna was married to actor Sean Penn, who at the time was best known for his role as Jeff Spicoli in the movie *Fast Times at Ridgemont High*.

1985, Madonna was still empire-building, branching out in as many directions as her talent and ambition would take her. A full-scale, nationwide concert tour, The Virgin Tour, immediately sold out in twenty-eight major cities. Appearances in charity concerts such as Live-Aid, which benefited AIDS awareness, were planned. She would not allow for the fever pitch of her career to accommodate motherhood until the birth of her daughter Lourdes, a full decade later. However, by the end of the summer, Madonna would marry into a Hollywood family.

Mr. Right turned out to be actor/director Sean Penn. Penn established himself as one of the most talented and rebellious stars of the 1980s in popular teen movies such as *Taps*, *Fast Times at Ridgemont High*, and the *Falcon and the Snowman*. In a 2005 interview for Britain's *Now* magazine he remarked, "I wouldn't comfortably call myself a rebel, but there is a certain necessary level of dissatisfaction that's important, because to be complacent is creatively criminal. It's a constant struggle to find your own voice and to be loyal to it."[3]

"I've been popular and unpopular successful and unsuccessful loved and loathed and I know how meaningless it all is. Therefore I feel free to take whatever risks I want." — Madonna

Penn and Madonna met on the set of the *Material Girl* video through mutual friends, Mary Lambert and James Foley, who would later direct Madonna in the comedy *Who's That Girl?* and in several videos from her *True Blue* album, including "Live to Tell" and "Papa Don't Preach." In many ways, the Madonna/Penn pairing represented a culture clash of East versus West. Whereas Madonna enjoyed glamour, fashion, and an urbane social life, she described Penn as a "cowboy poet," a rugged, outdoorsy individualist. Hard drinking, chain smoking, short-tempered … in contrast, Madonna's upbeat, life-affirming persona held none of these somewhat self-destructive tendencies. Furthermore, the straightforward Penn had little patience for the spirited antics and sexual ambiguity of Madonna's East Coast friends. Yet what he did share

Because of their combined star status, Madonna and husband Sean
Penn were frequently followed by paparazzi throughout the 1980s.

with them was a passion for art and the courage to take creative risks.

The fact that their whirlwind romance coincided with the rapid upswing in Madonna's popularity contributed to its undoing. Though not yet the icon she is today, candid photographers, or paparazzi, were constantly on hand to photograph her every move. It was difficult to travel in any youth circle in 1985 without seeing evidence of her mass appeal. For example, Madonna kicked off her first concert tour at the Paramount Theatre in Seattle. Teenage fans, dubbed "Madonna wannabe's," flocked to this concert dressed like her. A performance review in *Rolling Stone* magazine claimed that "at least 80 percent of the girls in the crowd had [tried] their [hardest] to mimic their idol's looks, from bleaching and tousling their hair to wearing such Madonna-associated items as see-through blouses and crucifix earrings."[4]

Poison Penns

In July 1985, Penn proposed to Madonna in Nashville, the location of his movie *At Close Range.* They set a wedding date of August 16, Madonna's twenty-seventh birthday. The ceremony was a nightmare because the paparazzi invaded their Malibu wedding.

Despite precautions, photographers and cameramen surrounded the home and tried to infiltrate it. Even Madonna, who typically welcomed such fanfare, displayed her annoyance by giving the finger to the camera while Penn stuck his head up her dress.[6] The press had already dubbed the pair the "Poison Penns" because of Penn's periodically violent reaction to tabloid activity. Reporters

PLAYING DRESS-UP

The video for "Dress You Up," featuring live footage of the Detroit leg of her Virgin Tour, captures the "Madonna wannabe" fan phenomenon. Its long opening sequence focuses on excited fans happily entering the concert venue. As the music begins, Madonna, clad in a loud green and purple mini skirt and a multicolored paisley jacket, enthusiastically prances toward a sea of audience clones dressed nearly as flamboyantly as she is. "I thought it was amazing," Madonna remarked in hindsight, "amazing that a certain way I chose to look and dress became an obsession."[5]

held their ground, and helicopter noise compromised the ceremony.

Tension among the guests also marred the day. There was a sharp division between old money and new, the Hollywood crowd (Cher, Tom Cruise, Rosanna Arquette, Christopher Walken, and the Sheen Family) mixing uneasily with the New York contingent (including Andy Warhol, Erica Bell, Keith Haring, and Debi Mazar). Sibling rivalry added to the chaos. Maid of Honor Paula Ciccone, Madonna's look-alike younger sister, threw a tantrum at the reception proclaiming, "This should have been my wedding day, not hers ... All this attention should have been mine."[7]

Penn seemed to hit rock bottom during his four-year marriage to Madonna. While distinguishing himself as a murderer in *At Close Range* and a hotheaded cop in *Colors*, these extreme characters underscored the violence in his own life. His most publicized role became that of bodyguard husband. Headlines chronicled his reckless driving, assault charges, and verbal abuse of Madonna and her friends. In 1987 he served a month-long sentence in an L.A. County jail after repeatedly violating probation.

Although they divorced in 1989, Madonna and ex-husband Sean Penn have remained good friends. They're shown here at a charity gala put on by Penn in 2016.

Madonna pressed domestic assault charges against him, but dropped them after filing for divorce in 1989.

In an interview given shortly before their divorce, Madonna expressed more sadness than regret about the demise of her marriage. "I have great respect for him," she said. "It's like most relationships that fail. It's not one thing; it's many things that go on over a period of time."[8] In Penn's opinion, their differing attitudes toward fame and artistic integrity strained their union. "I never liked being under the spotlight," he said. "She was in the process of becoming the biggest star in the world. I just wanted to make my films and hide."[9]

Despite marital difficulties, Madonna remained focused and prolific, coproducing her *True Blue* album in 1986, which she dedicated to her husband's "very pure vision of love" by naming it after one of his favorite expressions.[10] *True Blue* garnered serious attention from music critics who believed it signaled "her transition from pop star to pop artist."[11] Critic Robert Hilburn remarked of the album, "Madonna visualizes music so that her best work seems equally designed with the stage or screen in mind—not just the jukebox."[12]

In 1987 she released *Who's That Girl?*, her first soundtrack album, named for her latest film and her first worldwide concert tour. This tour was more polished and theatrical than her first one, and spotlighted her new look—a short, tomboyish hairdo and firmer, athletic figure. There had never before been "a more forceful showcase for the feminine sensibility in pop."[13] "Madonna is simply the first female entertainer who has starred in a show of this scope," wrote Mikal Gilmore of *Rolling Stone* magazine. He described her ninety-minute tour-de-force as "a fusion of Broadway style choreography and post-

"PAPA DON'T PREACH"

One of *True Blue*'s hit songs, "Papa Don't Preach," tackles the issue of teenage pregnancy. Its video featured Madonna as an unwed mother-to-be from a working class home stalwartly deciding to keep her baby. Actor Danny Aiello, famous for his role as Tony Rosato in the Godfather movies, plays a sympathetic father who eventually accepts her situation. The video caused a stir, with some believing it encouraged teen pregnancy and others a pro-life message. Madonna is a pro-choice advocate.

disco song and dance that tops the standards set by live concert firebrands like Prince and Michael Jackson."[14]

Madonna's career was definitely on a roll. "She doesn't rest," noted *Who's That Girl?* costar Coati Mundi speaking about her frantic work ethic. "She was doing the movie, and the soundtrack album for the movie, and also planning her Who's That Girl? tour at the same time. She's doing all this stuff, plus she's got the lead in the film!"[15] Just as Penn's artistry received a boost after their divorce (he would soon star in a succession of powerful movies including *Casualties of War* and *State of Grace*) Madonna's next album, *Like a Prayer*, became widely recognized as one of her most accomplished offerings.

I Can Feel Your Power

Critics, biographers, and academics alike, view the accomplishment of her *Like a Prayer* album as the zenith of Madonna's career. *Like a Prayer* was perceived as an ambitious, confessional record covering universal themes, in which "Madonna is brutally frank about the dissolution of her marriage, her ambivalence toward her father and even her feelings of loss about her mother."[1]

Madonna seemed to feel that the time was right to reveal the vulnerable, spiritual side of her nature. "I didn't try to candy coat anything or make it more palatable for mass consumption, I guess," she said. "I wrote what I felt."[2] Throughout the album, she lays bare her feelings about her relationships with family and loved ones. Songs like "Till Death Do Us Part," convey the sense that Madonna used the album as therapy, working through the trauma of her broken marriage in order to move on with her life. Conflicted feelings and loyalties crop up in this song. People you love and who love you can hurt you the most. We push each other away in spite of ourselves. She hints at the positive aspects of self-examination. "The overall emotional context of the album is drawn from what I was going through when I was growing up," she explained, "and I'm still growing up."[3]

Madonna's performances frequently spark controversy, from her bumping and grinding during "Like a Virgin" to the religious iconography used in "Like a Prayer."

Tension between the sacred and the profane ultimately pulled focus away from the more blatantly self-revelatory songs in the album. Flirtation with religious iconography, including puns on her name, had been a part of Madonna's image since she first appeared on the music scene. She has admitted to consciously appropriating religious symbols such as crucifixes and rosaries, wearing them and toying with them, in order to demystify them." [4]

Coming to terms with her childhood while developing this album meant coming to terms with the Catholic faith in which she was raised. My "sense of art, drama, and

A SPIRITED DEBATE

Madonna frequently connects spirituality with sexuality in her work. "I'm very immersed in [how they are] not supposed to go together," she says, "but in my world they go together."[5] Though Christianity places them in conflict with each other, she sees this separation as detrimental. "That's why everyone has affairs and they cheat on their wives or their husbands. They have someone they idolize, and then they idolize them so much that they put them on a pedestal. And then they have to find [other] people to have fun with and get low-down and dirty."[6]

decadence all came from church. So did [my] sense of the power of secrets that lie in all the dark corners," Madonna said.[7]

Her "Like a Prayer" video centers on transformation and redemption and evokes medieval passion plays, a tradition of religious theater in churches. Although just a few minutes long, it has a complex plot resembling a criminal melodrama. A girl (Madonna) witnesses an assault and then the mistaken arrest of a black man. Conflicted, and afraid of getting involved, she enters a church where she wrestles with her conscience. Experiencing religious rapture akin to sexual rapture, she conquers her fears and helps free the man from jail. At the end of the video the performers bow, and a curtain closes.

During her Blond Ambition tour in 1990, Madonna focused on combining music and fashion, hoping to create a new kind of concert experience for her fans.

When the video was made, Madonna negotiated a five million dollar sponsorship deal with Pepsi-Cola Company for a commercial featuring the same song. Even though the commercial and the video had vastly different themes, fundamentalist Christian groups, such as the American Family Association, confused the two. They proclaimed the video blasphemous and threatened to boycott Pepsi-Cola products. Confronted by this pressure, Pepsi canceled her ads.

If religious factions and corporate America took exception to the work, academia found it exceptional. Madonna studies became a fad on college campuses. In 1992, for example, classes using Madonna works as text spanned English, women's studies, contemporary culture, and musicology curriculums at Rutgers, Harvard, and the University of California. Camille Paglia, professor of Humanities at University of the Arts in Philadelphia, maintained that with the video "Like a Prayer," "Madonna has made a major contribution to the history of women. She has rejoined and healed the split halves of woman: Mary, the Blessed Virgin and holy mother, and Mary Magdalene, the harlot."[8]

Live Out Your Fantasies Here with Me

In 1990, Madonna mounted a provocative new worldwide tour, Blond Ambition. By now seasoned at touring, she wanted to break all the rules. "The biggest thing we tried to do is change the shape of concerts," choreographer Vincent Patterson is quoted as saying. "Instead of just presenting songs, we wanted to combine fashion, Broadway, rock and the performance arts."[9] Striving for worldwide domination, the tour played twenty-seven cities in three continents in just over four months. The centerpiece of the set was a hydraulic platform, which Madonna descended at the beginning of the show, singing her crotch-grabbing anthem of empowerment and self-respect "Express Yourself." For the number, Madonna donned a tailored suit and monocle. Underneath she revealed industrial armor of another nature—a stunning cone-shaped bustier designed by Jean-Paul Gaultier.

Madonna wasn't the only one who wore lingerie during the show. In some numbers male tour members danced suggestively with each other and wore bullet bras. When asked if her fan base was sophisticated enough to digest this progressive sexual statement, Madonna replied, "They digest it on a lot of different levels. Some people will see it and be disgusted by it, but maybe they'll be unconsciously challenged by the idea of men in women's lingerie. Then there are people who see it and are amused by the irony of it. If people keep seeing it and seeing it, eventually it's not going to be such a strange thing."[10]

Not everyone was willing to embrace this mix of self-assertion, sexual freedom, and interrelationships. Officials in Toronto threatened to arrest Madonna if she didn't change the show. She refused, but they didn't press charges. When the Vatican spoke out against it, Madonna rallied. Proud of her Italian heritage, she staged a press conference defending her artistic vision. "My show is a theatrical presentation of my music," she told reporters. "Like theatre, it asks questions, promotes thought, and takes you on an emotional journey. I don't endorse a way of life but I describe one. The audience is left to make its own judgements. That's what I consider freedom of speech, expression, and thought."[11]

Her tour coincided with the release of her album *I'm Breathless*, linked to the Warren Beatty movie *Dick Tracy*; a stylized, action-comedy based on Chester Gould's 1930s detective comic strip. In the movie, Madonna plays bad-girl love interest Breathless Mahoney, a sexy nightclub singer and gangster's moll. Broadway composer Stephen Sondheim wrote three show tunes for her Breathless character, the style of which forms the basis for the rest of the torch songs in the album. Their urbane lyrics and intricate compositions represented a departure for Madonna, yet she proved she was capable of handling the musical theater genre. Her confident renditions foreshadow the virtuosity she would later display in the filmed version of the opera *Evita*.

"Vogue" appeared in the new tour and album. The only disco tune in *I'm Breathless*, the song refers to an evolution of break-dancing that involves striking various physical poses. Generally practiced in gay nightclubs by African and Latino males, vogue dancers form collectives called "Houses" that perform together. Madonna learned about vogueing from her actor/dancer friend Debi Mazar while she was developing her Blond Ambition stage show and looking for street dancers to work with. "Debi told me [about] Luis Ninja who's a spokesperson for the House of Extravaganza," she said. "He brought the whole House of Extravaganza, and they performed for me. They had the lights going, this music pumping. It was just the best dancers you've ever seen, and they were all freestyling."[12]

Madonna has been accused of "embodying the white mainstream's commercial appropriation and watering down of traditionally African-American music."[13] Feminist and racial scholar Bell Hooks is especially critical of Madonna's method of borrowing from African-

Madonna's Blond Ambition tour would go on to inspire pop singers to do more than simply sing and dance. Each song became a carefully choreographed stage show.

American influences and profiting from them. "It's a very recent historical phenomenon for any white girl to be able to get some mileage out of flaunting her fascination and envy of blackness," she writes in an essay in which she likens Madonna to a plantation mistress.[14]

These accusations extend to her appropriation of the gay lifestyle, which some have argued undermines alternative gender politics. In the essay "No Sex in Sex," professors Donald Crimp and Michael Warner chide Madonna for using the queer aesthetic as a foil to eroticize and glamorize her own image, contending that "Madonna can be as queer as she wants to, but only because we know she's not."[15] Grudgingly, they admit that Madonna's attempts to normalize what others perceive as subversive sexual behaviors have not only challenged heterosexuals, but have helped to unite the homosexual community. "Appropriation is a weird term," Warner writes, "because in a way you always win these battles by being appropriated."[16]

Madonna's identification with homosexuals is not disingenuous. As Professor Crimp points out, "She certainly hangs out with queers enough to have adopted queer style for herself."[17] Her dance mentor, Christopher Flynn, was gay, as is her brother Christopher and many of her friends including comedienne Sandra Bernhard, artist Andy Warhol, and nightclub owner Ingrid Casares. Videos for her songs "Justify My Love" and "Erotica" were banned or censored for their explicit content, including portrayal of cross-dressing, sadomasochism, and homosexuality.

In 1991, Madonna told *The Advocate* magazine that she felt a lot of camaraderie with the gay community and their feelings of persecution and being an outsider. "I'm completely compassionate about their choice in life, their

AIDING A CAUSE

From the beginning of her career, Madonna championed gay rights at a time when it wasn't chic to do so. In the earliest stages of the AIDS epidemic, when little was known about its cause, it was labeled a "homosexual" disease and AIDS victims were shunned. Madonna campaigned actively for AIDS awareness. Having lost many close friends to AIDS, she's donated millions of dollars to projects such as the American Foundation for AIDS Research. A vocal proponent of safe sex, she's been known to add condoms to the per diem pay of employees.

life-style, and I support it," she stated.[18] Her empathy is evident in the tell-all documentary of her Blond Ambition tour, *Truth or Dare*. The film "is about more than music. It is about what it takes and what it means to be a star. ... it comes as close as any movie can to capturing her [Madonna's] essence."[19]

Madonna allowed director Alek Keshishian complete access onstage and off, to chronicle the experience of life on the road with her and her entourage. She encouraged him and his camera crew to be intrusive and unsparing as they probed the behind-the-scenes drama that unfolded as the tour progressed. The result does not always flatter its subject matter. We see a spectrum of Madonnas— generous to insensitive, companionable to vulgar. "It is extremely realistic. It is Madonna as I know her," commented her brother Christopher.[20]

Some reviewers expressed concern for the plight of the tour dancers "whose vulnerability she admits to exploiting in order to play the mother-figure."[21] Others held another view. They found the documentary innovative, praising it for its ground-breaking perspective of gay culture. "It's hard to think of another film about a non-gay subject in which the presence of gay people is not only normal and accepted but treasured. Of her seven dancers, all are ethnic minorities, and all but one are gay. Madonna clearly identifies with them, camping and partying and flirting with them freely."[22]

Three of the dancers sued Madonna over the movie. When asked if she'd gone too far or revealed too much, Madonna attributed this attitude to general overreaction to her work. "Life is about the highs and the lows, and if you just present the mids, then what's the point?" she explained.[23]

Never Forget Who You Are

Madonna's next move was to form her own multimedia enterprise, Maverick Entertainment. It enabled Madonna, as CEO, to develop her own books, records, videos, and related merchandise. Maverick's first venture was *Sex*, a partly autobiographical coffee table book written by Madonna. In diary format, she takes on the character of Mistress Dita (based on Dita Parlo, a silent movie actress). "This book is about sex," Dita pens. "Sex is not love. Love is not sex. But the best of both worlds is created when they come together… Everything you are about to see and read is a fantasy, a dream, pretend."[1]

One hundred and twenty-eight photos accompany the text, shot by Steven Meisel, who had collaborated with Madonna on fashion magazine spreads. He photographed her alone and in compromising positions with pizza slices, gasoline pumps, skinheads, and male strippers. Celebrities such as Vanilla Ice, Naomi Campbell, Isabella Rossellini, and Big Daddy Kane also posed with her.

Spiral bound between sheets of metal, sheathed in mylar with added goodies such as an "Erotica" song sampler and a comic book, *Sex* cost fifty dollars. Marketed as an art book, it sold in regular bookstores. This outraged a mix of people worldwide. *Sex* was condemned as

In 1993, fresh off the release of her *Erotica* album and *Sex* book, Madonna staged the Girlie Show tour, which featured more of her patented choreography and costumes.

pornography and banned in several states and countries. The backlash against Madonna included hate mail and death threats.

Maverick weathered the criticism surprisingly well. *Sex* sold 150,000 copies on its first day of release in the United States and 500,000 the first week. One and a half million copies sold around the globe, generating a net profit of almost twenty million dollars. The maverick behind Maverick considered it a turning point in her career.

After the scandal of *Sex*, Madonna produced chart-topping albums such as *Erotica* and *Bedtime Stories*. Maverick Records also signed top-notch performers like Alanis Morissette. *Dangerous Game*, the first movie financed by her production company, attracted seasoned veterans Harvey Keitel, James Russo, and director Abel Ferrara. *The New York Times* gave the experimental film a positive review, calling it a "scorching psychodrama." They noted Madonna's demure performance.[2]

In 1993, Madonna launched the Girlie Show, a cabaret tour staged like a circus. In Girlie Show, Madonna reprised her Dita character, serving as Mistress of Ceremonies throughout the two-hour burlesque. She set the tone in the opening act, brandishing a ringmaster's whip while topless acrobats performed a pole dance.

EVA PERÓN

Madonna identified with the real-life Evita. Born in poverty, through drive and ambition she transformed herself into a glamorous radio star who, like Madonna, hungered for mass adulation. It was in the political arena, however, that she gained her fame after marrying Perón. Her popularity and identification with the working class helped secure him the presidency in 1946. Their regime was suspect. Perón and Evita lived an extravagant lifestyle, hoarding nearly as much money as they lavished on the poor through lotteries and work projects. Evita died of ovarian cancer in 1952 at the age of thirty-three.

Those who missed the humor in her *Sex* book could not fail to catch the parody and exaggeration in this decadent show.

Though Girlie Show was a sellout around the world, Madonna sought a meatier comeback. She pursued the starring role in the film version of Andrew Lloyd Webber and Tim Rice's 1978 rock opera *Evita*, based loosely on the life of Evá Perón (Evita), the wife of Argentinian dictator Juan Perón.

Director Alan Parker was reluctant to cast Madonna in the movie, given her less than stellar reputation at the box office. Rice championed her, however, aware that her look, personality, and singing and dancing talent made for

In 1996, Madonna starred in *Evita*, the biographical movie musical based on the life of Argentina's most famous first lady, Eva Perón. Madonna won a Golden Globe for her performance.

a more plausible Evita than the bevy of screen actresses up for the role. "I think she's a fine artist and I was very keen for her to get the part," he said.[3]

Madonna poured herself into the role, studying Evita's life and affecting her mannerisms. Since the movie is an opera, with complex musical arrangements and virtually no speaking lines, she took singing lessons and learned how to dance the tango. Her efforts paid off handsomely. She carried the movie, receiving a Golden Globe Award for her strong performance.

Though extremely rewarding, making the movie proved arduous for Madonna. Evita was filmed in three countries—Argentina, Britain, and Hungary—and paparazzi followed her everywhere. In Argentina the project was unpopular. She was harassed by protesters offended that she was cast in the role of their national hero "When we were in Argentina," confirmed Evita costar Antonio Banderas, "half of the people were hating her, and half of the people were loving her. It was really the story all over again of Evá Duarte [Perón's maiden name]."[4]

Never Forget Who You Are, Little Star

Near the end of the filming, Madonna discovered that she was pregnant. "I felt that it was kind of poetic that it happened while I was trying to give birth to another sort of baby," she told a reporter. [5] Since her divorce, Madonna's love life had been a circus. She juggled celebrity boyfriends such as Warren Beatty with employee conquests such as her bodyguard Jim Albright. Her current love was a suave Manhattan personal trainer and actor named Carlos Leon. The two met while jogging in Central Park. Before her pregnancy, theirs had been a low-key love affair. The pregnancy was unplanned but both were excited by the prospect of parenthood. At thirty-eight, Madonna was eager to have a child. On October 14, 1996, she gave birth to daughter Lourdes Maria Ciccone Leon.

Despite accusations that Carlos Leon was merely a "sperm donor," he and Madonna had dated for two years before her pregnancy and seemed very content with each other. But though Carlos Leon maintains a significant presence in Lourdes's life, he didn't remain Madonna's beau for long. Madonna settled with Lourdes in California, and Leon's ties were in New York. They ended their relationship in 1997; parting company as good friends and coparents. Madonna then entered a very spiritual phase. "The whole idea of giving birth and being responsible for another life put me in a different place," she said at the time. "I feel like I'm starting my life over in some ways. My daughter's birth was like a rebirth for me."[6]

Madonna told talk-show host Larry King that being a mother was more than what she thought it would be. "Every day I am in complete wonderment of her ... I love looking into her eyes. I love watching her grow. I love watching her absorb life around her."[7]

Motherhood seemed to deepen Madonna's serenity and her artistic convictions. According to Ingrid Sischy of *Vanity Fair* magazine, "Having a baby gave her what she calls 'a moment of stillness' when she was forced to allow herself to slow down, step away, and surrender."[8] *Ray of Light*, released in 1998, embodied this new inner calm. During production, Madonna left herself open to experimentation. Desiring to update her dance tunes with an ethereal sonic texture she couldn't achieve with

SPIRITUAL AWAKENING

Madonna's spiritual journey also influenced the album. Although Madonna was raised Catholic, she rejected many of its principles. Her interest in spiritual philosophy, though, had never waned. Through the years, she had studied Eastern religions such as Hinduism and Buddhism. While pregnant with Lourdes, she began practicing yoga and Kabbalah, an ancient Jewish doctrine that promotes unity and inner harmony. Her yogic practices led her to study Sanskrit, a language she uses in the song "Shanti/Ashtangi."

live musicians, she chose to collaborate with British musician and producer William Orbit, an underground electronic artist.

Unlike the past, she entered the studio without a set idea of what the music would sound like. Madonna stated, "I let William [Orbit] play Mad Professor. He comes from a cutting-edge sort of place—he's not a trained musician, and I'm used to working with classically trained musicians—but I knew that's where I wanted to go. Oftentimes the creative process was frustrating because I wasn't used to it; it took longer than usual to make this record. But I realize now that I needed that time to get where I was going."[9]

Orbit's electronic sound perfectly married the themes of rebirth, redemption, mysticism, and spirituality that Madonna wanted to explore through the album. She had been listening to world music including North African and Indian music, so Orbit programmed Eastern instruments such as the sitar, rebana, and tabla into the recordings.

The result was a critical and commercial triumph, securing Madonna artistic accolades and four Grammy Awards. She followed her success with *Music*, working again with Orbit as well as French producer Mirwais Ahmadzai. Her new synth-heavy, technology-driven musical direction earned Madonna the title "Veronica Electronica." Veronica is Madonna's confirmation name, the name she chose for herself as a preteen when she underwent the Roman Catholic sacrament of verifying her membership in the church.

In 1998, Madonna was still an unwed mother. Lyrics from *Ray of Light*'s, "Has To Be," speak of her yearnings for a soul mate. They assert her belief that she would connect with someone who existed in the world just for her. She was right, of course, and "Veronica Electronica" would soon meet the man whose name she was destined to step out with.

That same year, Trudi Styler, wife of legendary rock vocalist Sting, coproduced the independent film about British gangsters, *Lock, Stock and Two Smoking Barrels*. In the summer, she invited Madonna, a long-time friend, to visit her at her English residence to discuss a possible soundtrack album. She arranged for the film's director, Guy Ritchie, to sit next to Madonna at lunch. Though Madonna's involvement in the soundtrack album didn't pan out, a romance between her and Ritchie did.

Madonna gave birth to her first child, daughter Lourdes, in October 1996. The birth of Lourdes would inspire many songs on Madonna's next album, *Ray of Light*.

Guy Ritchie immediately captured Madonna's interest. For Madonna, it was love at first sight. Ruggedly handsome and ten years her junior, he apparently stopped her in her tracks. After their first meeting, she later said, "I went into a state of denial because he lived here and I lived in America and I wasn't interested in torturing myself by having some long-distance love affair. But it happened anyway. It was just one of those … inexplicable uncontrollable things."[10]

Despite a rocky start—an on again/off again battle of wills—she committed herself to him. His independent nature, coupled with his willingness to resist her domination, made him irresistible to her. Several tracks on her *Music* album, particularly "Amazing" and "I Deserve It," were essentially love songs to Ritchie. They refer to the destiny of two people's lives converging upon each other.

Ritchie refused to leave Europe, where his career was centered. Therefore, in 2000, Madonna uprooted her entourage and moved to London. She was willing to sacrifice to make things work for all involved, scheduling transatlantic visits so that she could maintain her business interests in the states, and so Lourdes could spend time with her father. "There are many days when I feel like a stranger in a strange land and I despair," Madonna nevertheless said of her move. "I miss my friends and I miss certain things that one always misses about the country of their origin. But I love the idea—whether it's in my work or where I live—exploring new frontier."[11]

9

This Guy Was Meant for Me

O n August 11, 2000, Madonna gave birth to Rocco, her son by Ritchie. Madonna returned home with the baby on her forty-second birthday to find a paper bag lying atop her nightstand. A gift box with a diamond ring and a marriage proposal was inside. "He wrote to me about everything we've been through, my birthday and the baby and how happy he was," recalled Madonna.[1]

Four months later Rocco was baptized in a thirteenth-century cathedral in Dornoch, Scotland. The next day, on December 22, 2000, Madonna and Ritchie exchanged wedding vows in Scotland's Skibo Castle. Thanks to private security, the ceremony was a grand and uninterrupted one. Two best men represented Ritchie—film producer Matthew Vaughan and London nightclub owner Piers Adam. Stella McCartney, daughter of Paul McCartney, designed Madonna's ivory silk wedding gown, and was maid of honor. Lourdes served as flower girl.

After her picture perfect wedding, Madonna set out once again to conquer the world. Her Drowned World Tour played forty-eight cities in arena stages around the globe and featured songs on her *Ray of Light* and *Music* albums. Madonna's presence in this tour is noticeably defiant. She replaces the camp of her other shows with rock star attitude and avant-garde self-consciousness.

Madonna with ex-husband Guy Ritchie and her two biological children, Rocco and Lourdes, in 2007. The couple divorced a year later, after adopting a son, David.

Through her stark lyrics, belligerent electric guitar solos, in-your-face banter, and violent choreography, she sets out "to intimidate the audience as much as to entertain them," wrote one reporter.[4] "I feel that the 'Drowned World' tour was a statement of who she had evolved into," tour director and choreographer Jamie King articulated. "You had to have that dark version, a very introspective and heavy version of her, to be able to get to this next place which was the Re-Invention tour."[5]

Madonna's Re-Invention tour took place three years later in 2004 and netted her $125 million. It seemed to mark a return to a more fan-friendly performance with much less distance between Madonna and her audience.

LOVE ON THE DANCE FLOOR

Guests described Madonna as looking "like a princess" in an antique lace veil held in place by an Edwardian diamond tiara.[2] The guest list read like a celebrity who's who, among them Sting, Trudi Styler, Gwyneth Paltrow, Rupert Everett, Donatella Versace, Carlos Leon, and members of the bride and groom's family. They feasted on lobster, salmon, and Aberdeen angus beef, then toasted the bride and groom. Later, the bridal party and guests danced in the castle basement, set up as a disco. The DJ, Miami's Tracy Young, who would later remix Madonna albums *Music* and *Confessions on a Dance Floor*, spun hits by Sting and Madonna.[3]

Enormous screens projected Madonna and her dancers live, but also played prerecorded dance routines that complemented the onstage action. Suspended catwalks allowed Madonna to venture out into the crowd. King explains this flip-flop in tone as follows: "Madonna is a true artist. She has to be able to explore and become what she is at that moment. She was the Re-Invention Tour at the time of the Re-Invention Tour. She was the Drowned World Tour at the time of that tour."[6]

Songwriter Joe Henry, Madonna's brother-in-law, once aptly likened the quick pace of Madonna's concerts to a parade. For Re-Invention, King designed the staging and choreography to specifically reflect perpetual motion. He wanted to give the impression of continual progression—one surprise after the other. "One minute she's provocatively vogueing with her male dancers, the next she's in fatigues, twirling a rifle to the sounds of explosions and helicopters," relayed a reporter covering the tour's kick-off.[7] According to fan Matthew Hunt, "The show was a sensory overload, with constant video projections, a moving stage, fire-jugglers, break-dancers, and skateboarders."[8]

It was also retrospective, re-examining hits spanning Madonna's career from a post-9/11 perspective, including her single "American Life." In this rap ditty, she questions the shallowness of modern life and the American Dream under President George W. Bush's conservative watch. Before the tour, this song had generated a lot of controversy given the tense political climate of the United States, embroiled in an unpopular conflict with Iraq. Intended "to convey strong anti-war, anti-materialism and anti-fashion industry statements,"[9] the American Life video proliferated with militaristic images—flags, fighter jets, mushroom clouds. Soldiers and refugees model fashion fatigues as they strut down a runway. At the end, Madonna tosses a fake grenade to a George Bush look-alike who uses it to light his cigar.

The Re-Invention tour was so-named to poke fun at Madonna's many incarnations.

She was now a happily married wife with two children. Besides being a diva, she ran a tidy business and home life. "Even my children have to clean up their mess, clean up their rooms," she is quoted as saying. "Manners, 'thank you,' 'please,' 'take your dishes to the sink.' I mean … gratitude, being grateful—that is—that has to happen."[10]

These traditional values included fostering her children's imaginations by encouraging them to read books instead of watching television. As a child, books such as *Alice in Wonderland*, *Charlotte's Web*, and *The Chronicles of Narnia* had been her fondest escape. Yet she wasn't satisfied with the content of most of the books they were reading.

Throughout her career, Madonna has been a prolific writer. She keeps a pillow book of ideas (a diary or journal), jotting down dreams or poems or things she

In 2004, Madonna, already well into her forties, embarked on her Re-Invention World Tour, proving that she still had as much star power as she had twenty years earlier.

reads in books. Pillow book in hand, with memories of the bedtime stories her father improvised for her and her eight siblings, she resolved to branch into children's fiction. Madonna contracted with Penguin Books to write her own series of five picture books. "I sit in front of the computer and stick my little statue, who's my writing muse, next to my computer and, OK, I'm going to write—and it comes," she explained of her writing process.[11]

In September 2003, her first children's book, *English Roses* was published in thirty languages and distributed in one hundred countries. It immediately topped the *New York Times* bestseller list. *Mr. Peabody's Apples*, *Yakov and the Seven Thieves*, and *The Adventures of Abdisoon* followed. *Lotsa de Casha*, her fifth, saw print in June 2005. All of Madonna's books are beautifully designed and illustrated. Her stories carry clear morals about the power of words or the importance of helping others.

Veteran children's authors such as Jane Yolen dismissed Madonna's efforts, unhappy that she'd joined the bandwagon of celebrity authors. "What really gripes me," Yolen complained, "is when someone like Madonna gets on national television and says [something like], 'I had to write my book because there weren't any good children's books out there.'"[12]

Marriage and motherhood had definitely altered Madonna's priorities. This is most evident when watching *Let Me Tell You a Secret*, the documentary of her Re-Invention tour. The film captures a mature and centered woman. It is the companion to *Truth or Dare*, which was made during her Blond Ambition tour. No longer "working out publicly [her] confusion about [her] own sexuality," Madonna has learned to differentiate between family and work, personal life and celebrity.[13]

"It's a different me," she said. "I have a husband, I have a family, my whole life has changed. It would be pretty strange if I was behaving the same way I did 12 years ago—that would be a little freaky."[14]

That said, in 2005 Madonna returned to the music of her childhood with her fourteenth album, *Confessions on a Dance Floor*, an homage to 1970s disco. Pounding beats and sassy lyrics married nostalgic tracks from disco groups ABBA and the BeeGees with remix technology that allowed Madonna to be her own backup singer. Her Confessions Tour the following summer resembled a theme party with lots of disco balls and dancing. "I'm going to turn the world into one big dance floor," she said.[15]

The tour proved to be another profitable venture for Madonna, demonstrating her continued worldwide popularity. However, it also showed that Madonna would not shy away from controversy as she approached the age of fifty. Madonna received criticism and calls for excommunication from members of the Roman Catholic Church in the United States, Europe, and Asia for a segment of her performance during which she staged a mock crucifixion. She descended to the stage on a glittered, mirrored, suspended cross while wearing a fake crown of thorns. Despite protests, Madonna would not change her show, even while performing roughly a mile from the Vatican when the tour reached Rome.

Love Spent

Madonna's major project in 2006 was humanitarian rather than music related. She endeavored to assist orphans in Malawi, Africa, a nation in the southeastern part of the continent plagued by AIDS and malaria.[16] Madonna aimed to raise at least three million dollars for the Raising Malawi project, which she and Kabbalah Center originator Michael Berg cofounded. She met with former President Bill Clinton to finance a one million dollar documentary about the difficulties facing the orphans. Finally, Madonna formed a partnership with Dr. Jeffrey Sachs, an antipoverty champion, to improve the health, agriculture, and economy of a Malawi village.[17]

"Now that I have children and what I consider to be a better perspective on life, I have felt responsible for the children of the world," Madonna said.[18] August 2006 witnessed the groundbreaking of an orphan-care center in Malawi capable of feeding and educating up to 1,000 children a day.[19] Subsequent relief projects she's helped finance in Malawi include hospitals such as the Mercy James Institute of Pediatric Surgery and Intensive Care, community based child care centers, and primary and secondary schools.[20]

In October of 2006, Madonna and Guy Ritchie adopted a baby from Malawi called David Banda. Ritchie has since remarked he had trepidations about this move, believing they should have spent more energy working on their marriage rather than expanding their family.[21] However, he did agree to this decision, and photos consistently portray Ritchie as a doting father.

David lived in an orphanage, but he wasn't an orphan. His biological father, Yohane Banda, didn't have the resources to care for David when his wife Marita died. Yohane's responses regarding the adoption have been contradictory. At one point he believed he would still be David's father and "the nice rich lady would simply be taking care of David for him and offering him a better life."[22] Due to African laws, the adoption wasn't formally

Madonna sits between two of her adopted children, David and Mercy, at a school in Malawi. The school was built by Raising Malawi, a charity started by Madonna to help Malawi's orphans.

confirmed until two years later in 2008. To the dismay of family-oriented government officials who believed David would have the stability of two parents in the home, shortly afterward, Madonna and Ritchie divorced.

There are interesting parallels between Madonna's first marriage to Sean Penn and her marriage to Guy Ritchie. Both couples collaborated on films with disastrous results. In 1986, newlyweds Madonna and Penn costarred in *Shanghai Surprise*, an adventure drama that was universally panned. Ritchie directed Madonna in *Swept Away*, in 2002. It likewise won many worst awards—Worst Director, Worst Screen Couple, Worst Remake.[25] Critic A.O. Scott of the *New York Times* disparaged Madonna's one-dimensional acting in *Swept Away*. "Striking a pose

CHOSEN FAMILY

Besides David, Madonna has adopted three other children from Malawi. Mercy James became her daughter in 2009. Twins Esther and Stella Mwale entered the family in 2017. All four children lost their real mothers in childbirth, so Madonna is the only mother they've known. Each still have family in Malawi. Mercy's family attempted to sue Madonna for failing to honor agreements about frequent visitation rights.[23] In 2016, Madonna lost a nine-month custody battle with ex-husband Ritchie over their biological son Rocco. Rocco left her Rebel Heart Tour in defiance of her strict rules to stay with his dad, who imposes fewer boundaries.[24]

is not the same as embodying a person, and a role like this one requires the surrender of emotional control, something Madonna seems constitutionally unable to achieve."[26]

Still, *Swept Away* was a family affair and behind-the-scenes videos highlight the couple's lighthearted moments. In between takes, they banter with each other and play with their children. Madonna can be seen bouncing baby Rocco on her knees. Ritchie perches Rocco upon a camera and flips him upside down to squeals of delight. He mischievously chases stepdaughter Lourdes on the beach—the movie was filmed on location in Malta and Sardinia.[27]

Both of Madonna's ex-husbands are quiet and reserved, preferring privacy and a normal family life. They chafed at the role of being married to such a famous and controlling woman. In an interview after their divorce, Ritchie said, "I want to be able to go about my life without all the hoopla. Unfortunately, she can't live without all the hoopla." He also believed that Madonna changed from being fun-loving to losing a sense of humor about herself. "She's obsessed with her own public image, obsessed with being seen as some kind of global soothsayer. It's silly; she's a pop star."[28]

Belittlement of this nature eroded their marriage. Ritchie purportedly called her a granny, unfavorably comparing her to young dancers she employed on tour. His remarks led Madonna to feel "incarcerated" because Ritchie didn't seem to understand that she takes her privileged position in the world seriously, as she does her continued development as an artist.[29] "That is one of the arguments I used to get into with my ex-husband, who used to say to me, "But why do you have to make another record? Why do you have to go on tour? Why do you have to make a movie? And I'm like, 'Why do I have to explain myself?'"[30]

Madonna has also publicly commented about her husband's emotional unavailability. She first detected a strain in her marriage after an accident in 2005, in which she fell off a horse and broke several bones. Madonna wanted Ritchie's care and support during her recovery, but according to her he became distant. "It was the beginning of her understanding that he wasn't a partner in every sense of the word,"[31] revealed friend Trudi Styler.

10

Veni, Vidi, Vici

The end of her marriage coincided with the Sticky & Sweet Tour, promoting her *Hard Candy* album. She performed in Boston on the night that her divorce was officially announced. Perhaps as a pointed nod to Ritchie, she included the wistful ballad "Miles Away." The lyrics read, "I guess we're at our best when we're miles away." Madonna insisted she was "tapping into the global consciousness of people who have intimacy problems" when she wrote this song.[1] It also seems to allude to her own marital problems; chiefly the literal and figurative long-distance relationship she and her husband sustained.

The Sticky & Sweet Tour was a "big, bombastic [commercial] success."[2] It remains the highest-grossing concert tour by a female artist and is on the list of the five top selling concert tours of all time. Madonna billed it as a "rock driven dancetastic journey" in four acts. The first catered to the erotic "Candy Shop," then morphed into the political hip hop of "4 Minutes." The second was classic Madonna, including "Into the Groove." The third appealed to the gypsy side of her, and featured a Romani folk trio that backed her on nostalgic tunes like "La Isla Bonita." The fourth act was an upbeat dance party, with crowd-pleasers such as "Ray of Light."

In 2008, Madonna went out on the Sticky & Sweet tour. The tour made $280 million, making it the highest-grossing tour by a solo artist at the time.

Madonna intentionally plans her shows with sections that highlight different characters and moods. "I take a lot of ideas and references from films or archetypal characters," she's explained. She pushes her dancers to try on distinct personas, too. "I force everyone to go outside their comfort zones. So straight boys wear high heels. And gay boys have to, you know, man up! I think it's important for everybody to understand that they're playing characters when they come into my realm and that they're telling stories."[3]

In the MDNA World Tour, Madonna sought to take her audience on "a journey of the soul from dark to light."[4] The first section is dark, indeed, with guns, blood splatters, gas masks, headstones, and creepy clown masks. On the Russian leg of the tour, she and her tour mates witnessed the growing fascist movement in Europe that prefigured the rise of the alt-right. At a concert for Amnesty International in 2014, Madonna spoke of her tour experience.

"I happened to be in Moscow the day that [a Russian girl band] went on trial for singing their song "Punk Prayer" in a church. This song criticized Vladimir Putin's regime and his blatant intolerance of human rights. I was shocked and outraged and I spoke about it openly during my show. For this, I received several death threats. From there we went to St. Petersburg where my show was being damned by the same regime for promoting homosexuality. All people working on my show, including myself, were threatened [with arrest]. Needless to say I did not change one moment. Unfortunately, 87 members of my audience were arrested for openly displaying gay behavior."[5]

The MDNA tour wasn't all grim foreboding. Each night the show paused so Madonna could directly address

Madonna hit the road on the MDNA tour in 2012. Although it was one of her most controversial tours, it was also one of her most successful, with eighty-eight sold-out performances.

the crowd. During a Miami performance, she thanked her fans and added, "You're all girls gone wild!" Then she asked them, "If you're really sure of who you are, it doesn't matter what people call you, does it? Because we know what's important is what's on the inside. You want to be a part of bringing peace to this world? You can start by treating the person next to you like a human being."[6] The crowd did go wild then, cheering and hugging each other.

Reviewers agree she had a breakthrough moment in this tour. Before resuming the aggressive focus of the show, by allowing a male dancer to violently lace her into a corset, Madonna sang a slow, intense waltz version of "Like a Virgin" that reminded one reviewer of a Brechtian cabaret. "I honestly did not suspect she had that performance in her," the reviewer opines. "It suggests that she might actually have somewhere creative to go as her pop appeal wanes."[7]

Madonna's *MDNA* album had received mixed reviews. Critics seemed to favor her collaborations with William Orbit on songs like "Falling Free," and "Masterpiece" over her experimental ditties. *The Village Voice* declared she's "almost a non-presence" in most of the album, which relegates her voice to the background in favor of grating sound effects, dubstep beats, and raps.[8] Yet Madonna found an ingenious way to market her album. Her appearance in the halftime show of the Super Bowl in 2012 was, "pure spectacle by the Cleopatra of the game," according to the *L.A. Times*; and a "shockingly transparent advertisement for *MDNA*."[9]

Naysayers didn't believe that at fifty-three Madonna would have the stamina, star power, and sex appeal to hold the attention of a super-sized crowd of sports fans.

A GOLDEN OPPORTUNITY

In 2012, Madonna won a Golden Globe Award for Best Original Song for "Masterpiece," part of the soundtrack of the movie *W.E.* During the MDNA tour, she sang an acoustic version while clips from the movie appeared onscreen. *W.E.* was the first feature film Madonna wrote and directed. It details the scandal caused when King Edward VIII abdicated the British throne to marry American divorcee Wallis Simpson. Their life together is revealed by a modern-day New Yorker who researches what she considers the ultimate love story. The *Guardian* summed up the movie in three words—"pretty but vacant."[10]

But for Madonna, performing at the Super Bowl was "a Midwesterner girl's dream."[11] She pulled out no stops, hiring multimedia studio Moment Factory and Cirque du Soleil, a high-tech circus, to create impressive visual supplements to the music and choreography. They utilized a technique called projection mapping, which transposes three-dimensional effects over physical spaces—in this case the football field at the Lucas Oil Stadium in Indianapolis. "Madonna's a perfectionist, and she wanted to do something extraordinary, so that was the objective of everybody," said Eric Fournier of Moment Factory.[12]

During Madonna's Super Bowl halftime show, "dazzling projections transformed the [stage and] field into a brand new visual environment, transitioning between scenes and songs with the flick of Madonna's wrist or a kick of her stilettoed leather boot."[13] A giant arcade-style boom-box accompanies "Music." Just before "Like a Prayer," the field looked like it was sucked into an alien vortex. During her unforgettable "Vogue" medley, "the floor appears to be made of hundreds of squares which flip over and morph into covers of *Vogue* magazine, an image of Madonna looking out from each of them."[14]

Super Bowl audiences aren't typically Madonna fans. Nonetheless, she seemed in her element. Jen Chaney of *Celebritology* wrote a mock play-by-play of her performance representative of those who routinely disparage Madonna. She picked apart her outlandish costumes, her over-rehearsed dancing, and the many celebrity invitees that she implied out-sang and upstaged Madonna.[15] Consensus, however, suggests that Madonna nailed the 12-minute TV spotlight, which set a Super Bowl halftime record of 114 million viewers. *Entertainment Weekly* called it a "joyous, openhearted" show.[16] MTV reported that, "Madonna ensured that all anyone would be talking about around the water cooler come Monday morning was her, whether or not you completely loved what she did."[17]

Deep Down in My Rebel Heart

Madonna launched her Rebel Heart tour in 2015. Compared to the overarching angst in the MDNA tour, its

The Rebel Heart tour opened in Montreal, Canada, in September 2015. It was Madonna's tenth tour and her ninth worldwide excursion and consisted of eighty-two performances.

content and execution was more relaxed. Her conception of having a rebel heart formed the central theme; that of "living for love, rising above, overcoming heartbreak."[18] Critics around the world noted the tour featured, "a kinder, gentler and happier Madonna."[19] They embraced the unexpectedness of her smiles, her playfulness, and her infectious spontaneity.

Most numbers boasted the spectacle of mini stage plays. The warrior sequence for "Iconic" featured costumes modeled after real samurai armor. For "Holy Water," a wittily irreverent juxtaposition between sexuality and religion was achieved with sets that included "a bacchanalian Last Supper, nuns gyrating on stripper polls and famous faces from Renaissance religious paintings projected on screen."[20]

Madonna proved, however, that she has the charisma and virtuosity to command the stage without backup dancers and effects. The show's warmer, intimate moments were well-received. She aimed at emotional truth with acoustic ballads such as "La Vie en Rose," "Ghosttown," and "True Blue," accompanied by ukulele.

It may be that she was able to evince a buoyant, personable touch because she'd exorcized the demons of her divorce with Ritchie, her estrangement with Rocco, and other disappointments in the tracks of her *Rebel Heart* album. Many are subtly autobiographic and apocalyptic—"Ghosttown," which is about rebuilding after an Armageddon; "Wash All Over Me," which may convey Madonna's uncertainties about her career; and "Joan of Arc," which exposes the insecurities and detachment strong-willed people mask in the face of public criticism.

Not long after wrapping up her Rebel Heart tour, Madonna took part in the Met Gala, a "night when all

MAKING HISTORY

Madonna is drawn to the story of medieval saint Joan of Arc and her bravery in the face of persecution. A brilliant strategist who successfully waged a holy war for France against Britain, she dared to impersonate a man to gain authority. The church punished her as a heretic. "In the face of death, she didn't back down. And that resonates with me. Women need female role models like that. There's not a lot."[21]

Madonna is willing to assume the mantle of female role model, with limits. In "Joan of Arc" she sings, "I'm not Joan of Arc, not yet." By this she means that although she's never shied away from acting on her convictions, "I'm not ready to be burned at the stake. That does really require an elevated soul, you know? When you are really, really ready to die for what you believe in."[22]

the celebrities in the land dress in the wildest and boldest frocks they can find."[23] The Met Gala is a fund-raising event that benefits the Metropolitan Museum of Art's Costume Institute in New York. Each year it focuses on a theme that coincides with an institute exhibit. Attendees try to outdo each other selecting clothing and accessories to match. In 2016, the theme was Manus v. Machina: Fashion in an Age of Technology.

The *Daily Mail* wasn't alone in labelling Madonna's bondage-themed dress a "rare fashion fail."[24] Others attacked her "scandalous" outfit, intimating she was too old to bare so much flesh. Her gown was custom-made by Givenchy (a Madonna favorite French fashion house).[25] It consisted of a black leather body suit open at the breasts and derriere. A sheer lace over-gown exposed her back side. In keeping with the gala theme of exploring haute couture in the machine age, she'd wound strips of black material around her legs and arms "inspired by the therapeutic kinesiology tape she wears for her fatigued muscles on tour."[26] Thigh high boots completed the look.

In defense of her ensemble, Madonna posted the following response on Instagram, in which she declared herself an unapologetic rebel, encouraging fans to join her fight for gender equality.

"When it comes to women's rights we are still in the dark ages. My dress at the Met Ball was a political statement as well as a fashion statement. The fact that people actually believe a woman is not allowed to express her sexuality and be adventurous past a certain age is proof that we still live in an ageist and sexist society. If you have a problem with the way I dress it is simply a reflection of your prejudice. I'm not afraid to pave the way for all the girls behind me!"[27]

CONCLUSION

*B*illboard honored Madonna with their Woman of the Year award in December 2016. She tailored her candid acceptance speech to the young women who were following in her footsteps. She explained to her audience that while preparing for the evening she'd pondered what it was to be a woman in the music business. "When I first started writing songs I didn't think about feminism."[1] She listed female artists like Aretha Franklin as inspirations, but admitted that her "real muse was David Bowie. He embodied male and female spirit, and that suited me. He made me think there were no rules, but I was wrong. There are no rules, if you're a boy. If you're a girl, you have to play the game."[2]

Madonna then described this game; the slippery double standard that women must navigate in a male-dominated world. She listed dos and don'ts. You can be beautiful and allow yourself to be objectified. You can't be too smart, have opinions outside of the norm, or own your sluttiness by sharing your sexual fantasies. She advised, "Be what men want you to be, but more importantly, be what women feel comfortable with you being around other men. And finally, do not age, because to age is a sin. You will be vilified, and you will definitely not be played on the radio."[3]

She recalled reading damning headlines about herself because she refused to play the game. "I remember wishing that I had a female peer that I could look to for support," she said. "[Feminists] said I set women back by objectifying myself. Oh, I thought. So, if you're a feminist you don't have sexuality. You deny it."[4]

Madonna has been named by *Billboard* as the top touring female artist of all time, earning more than $1.31 billion in touring revenue since her Blond Ambition tour.

Her solution was to become a different kind of feminist, one who is independent, recognizes male oppression, and sticks up for herself and other women rather than blanketly believing what men say about her. She urged her audience to begin appreciating their own worth and to forge strong female friendships. She ended by reiterating her thanks for those who supported her, and extending it to those who didn't. "To everyone who gave me hell and said I could not, that I would not, that I must not, your resistance made me push harder, made me the fighter that I am today."[5]

What is Madonna today? Madonna is most famous for being Madonna. From albums and tours, to movies, books, and merchandise, she represents big business. She is also an activist that finds it strange that the phrase "human rights" is part of the modern lexicon. "The right to be free, to love who we want to love, to be who we are, do we have to fight for that?"[6] She's paid the price for speaking out against discrimination throughout her career but persists because "we all have a moral obligation to stand up when anyone is being persecuted, whether it's down the street from us, or on the other side of the world."[7]

Finally, Madonna is an artist concerned about staying relevant and making an impact on the world. The purpose of art, in her opinion, is to respectfully challenge people's ideas and beliefs, a task she has committed herself to for over three decades. "People say that I'm so controversial," she declares, "but I think the most controversial thing that I have ever done is to stick around."[8]

CHRONOLOGY

1958 Madonna Louise Ciccone is born in Bay City, Michigan.

1963 Madonna's mother dies of cancer.

1978 Madonna drops out of college and moves to New York City.

1979 After studying dance, Madonna becomes a backup dancer for French disco artist Patrick Hernandez; she also forms her first band this year.

1982 Her first single, "Everybody," is released and reaches number three on *Billboard*'s dance club chart.

1983 Her self-titled debut album, *Madonna*, is released.

1984 Madonna attends the first-ever MTV Video Music Awards (VMAs), shocking the audience with her live performance of "Like a Virgin."

1985 Madonna becomes a full-fledged triple threat after starring alongside Rosanna Arquette in the movie *Desperately Seeking Susan*. She also marries actor Sean Penn this year.

1987 The Who's That Girl Tour introduces Madonna to an international audience; Pope John Paul II encouraged Catholics to boycott her stop in Italy.

1989 Madonna courts controversy with the music video for her single "Like a Prayer," which features a field of burning crosses and Madonna kissing a saint. She also divorces Sean Penn this year.

1990 Madonna stars in *Dick Tracy*. She also releases *The Immaculate Collection* album.

1991 The tour documentary *Truth or Dare* premieres, following Madonna and her crew on tour.

1992 Madonna stars in the girl-power baseball movie *A League of Their Own* alongside stars like Tom Hanks, Geena Davis, and Rosie O'Donnell. She starts her own music label, Maverick. Her coffee-table book, *Sex*, is released.

1994 Madonna appears on *The Late Show With David Letterman* and curses a whopping fourteen times.

1996 Madonna makes her largest film appearance ever, starring as Argentina's first lady Eva Perón in the movie *Evita*, for which she also recorded the soundtrack; she later wins a Golden Globe for her performance. She gives birth to her daughter Lourdes this year.

2000 With partner Guy Ritchie, Madonna welcomes son Rocco in August.

2003 Nearly twenty years after her debut VMA appearance, Madonna once again courts controversy with a wild live performance at the annual awards show.

2006 Madonna cofounds Raising Malawi, a nonprofit that seeks to help orphaned children from the impoverished African nation; she adopts son David from Malawi that year as well.

2009 Madonna adopts Mercy James from Malawi.

2012 Madonna's performance becomes the most-watched Super Bowl halftime show up to that point.

2017 Showing that her idea of girl power hasn't diminished, Madonna is a key speaker during the 2017 Women's March on Washington. She also adopts two more young girls from Malawi.

CHAPTER NOTES

Introduction

1. Roxane Gay and Arianne Phillips, "Madonna's Spring Awakening," *Harper's Bazaar*, January 10, 2017, http://www.harpersbazaar.com/culture/features/a19761/madonna-interview.

2. Lyndsey Matthews, "Here's the Full Transcript of Madonna's Speech at the Women's March," *Elle*, January 21, 2017, http://www.elle.com/culture/career-politics/news/a42336/madonnas-womens-march-speech-transcript.

3. Donald Trump, EXCLUSIVE: Donald Trump Blasts 'Disgusting Madonna,'" Video, *Sean Hannity*, Fox News Network, January 27, 2017.

4. Spencer Kornhaber. "How Madonna Gave Trump Ammo with a Cry for Peace," *Atlantic*, January 23, 2017, https://www.theatlantic.com/entertainment/archive/2017/01/madonna-trump-blow-up-the-white-house-womens-march-speech/514106.

5. *Madonna Sticky & Sweet Tour*, directed by Nathan Rissman and Nick Wickham, Warner Bros. Records Inc., 2010.

6. Ibid.

7. Ibid.

Chapter 1: What It Feels Like for a Girl

1. Denise Worrell, "Now: Madonna on Madonna," *Time*, May 27, 1985, http://www.time.com/time/archive/printout/0,23657,957025,00.html.

2. Joel D. Schwarz, "Virgin Territory: How Madonna Straddles Innocence and Decadence," *New Republic*, August 26, 1985, pp. 30–33.

3. Gavin Mueller, "Pop Playground: MTV VMA Wrap-up," *stylusmagazine.com*, September 2, 2003, http://www.stylusmagazine.com/article/pop_playground/the-2003-vma-wrap-up.htm.

4. Sarah Warn, "VMA's Madonna-Britney-Christina Kiss: Progress or Publicity Stunt?," September 2004, http://www.afterellen.com/TV/vmakiss.html.

5. Tucker Carlson, "Britney Would Not Kiss Another Woman Besides Madonna," September 4, 2003, http://www.cnn.com/2003/SHOWBIZ/Music/09/03/britney.spears.

6. "Madonna Says Daughter Asked If She Was Gay," Associated Press, March 6, 2006, http://www.mercurynews.com/mld/mercurynews/entertainment/gossip/14032911.htm.

7. Jennifer Egan, "You Don't Know Madonna," December 2002, http://www.jenniferegan.com/articles/2002_12_gq_madonna.html.

8. Ibid.

9. Gabriella, "Bubble Gum Princess Gone Serene Queen," NY Rock, August 1998, http://www.nyrock.com/interviews/madonna_int.htm.

10. Jay Jimenez, "Interview," *Next Magazine*.

11. Elizabeth Banks, "Billboard 'Woman of the Year' Madonna Gives Provocative Interview on Everything from 2016 Election to Ageism," *Billboard Magazine*, December 5, 2016, http://www.billboard.com/articles/events/women-in-music/7597392/madonna-billboard-woman-of-the-year-interview.

12. Britney Spears, "Madonna," *Rolling Stone*, http://www.rollingstone.com/news/story/_/id/5940017?rnd=1136314579859&has-player=true&version=6.0.11.847.

Chapter 2: Mother and Father

1. "News Archive: January 2005," *Madonnalicious.com*, http://www.madonnalicious.com/archive/january2005.html.

2. Denise Worrell, "Now: Madonna on Madonna," *Time*, May 27, 1985, http://www.time.com/time/archive/printout/0,23657,957025,00.html.

3. Andrew Morton, *Madonna* (New York, NY: St. Martin's Press, 2001), p. 104.

4. Ibid.

5. Jane Stevenson, "Madonna's Metamorphosis Complete," *Toronto Sun*, March 1, 1998, http://www.canoe.ca/AllPop -Madonna/cd_rayoflight2.html.

6. "Madonna and Child: The New Baby, the New Life," *Vanity Fair*, March 1998, http://www.fortunecity.com/tinpan /underworld/437/vf.htm.

7. Nicole Claro, *Madonna* (New York, NY: Chelsea House Publishers, 1998), p. 24.

8. Worrell.

9. "Madonna and Child: The New Baby, the New Life," *Vanity Fair*.

10. Steven Holden, "Madonna Goes Heavy on Heart," *New York Times*, June 29, 1986.

11. Claro, p. 26.

12. John Skow, "Madonna Rocks the Land: Sassy, brassy and beguiling, she laughs her way to fame," *Time*, May 1985, http://www.allaboutmadonna.com/press_1985_time.php.

Chapter 3: You Can Dance, for Inspiration

1. "Madonna and Child, The New Baby, The New Life," *Vanity Fair*, March 1998, http://www.fortunecity.com /tinpan/underworld/437/vf.htm.

2. Denise Worrell, "Now: Madonna on Madonna," *Time*, May 27, 1985, http://www.time.com/time/archive /printout/0,23657,957025,00.html.

3. Ibid.

4. Nicole Claro, *Madonna* (New York, NY: Chelsea House Publishers, 1998), p. 29.

5. "Vladimir Dokoudovsky (1919–1998)," http:// michaelminn.net/andros/biographies/dokoudovsky_ vladimir.htm.

6. Andrew Morton, *Madonna* (New York, NY: St. Martin's Press, 2001), p. 57.

7. Stephen Holden, "Madonna Goes Heavy on Heart," *New York Times*, June 29, 1986.

8. Morton, p. 164

9. Don Shewey, "Madonna: The Saint, the Slut, the Sensation," *Advocate*, 1991, http://www.donshewey.com/music_articles/madonna1.htm.

10. Ibid.

11. Ibid.

12. Barbara Victor, *Goddess: Inside Madonna* (New York, NY: Harper Collins, Inc., 2001).

13. Worrell.

14. Jennifer Dunning, *Alvin Ailey: A Life in Dance* (New York, NY: Da Capo Press, 1998), p. 275.

15. E. Jean Carroll, "Justify Your Love," *Elle*, February 2001, http://www.ejeanlive.com/madonna.htm.

16. Christopher Anderson, "Madonna Rising: The Wild and Funky Early Years in New York," *New York Magazine*, October 14, 1991.

17. Barbara Victor, *Goddess: Inside Madonna* (New York, NY: Harper Collins, Inc, 2001), p. 179.

18. Morton, p. 65

19. Victor.

Chapter 4: She's a Real Disco Queen

1. "Artist Biographies: Patrick Hernandez," Disco Museum website.

2. Ibid.

3. Andrew Morton, *Madonna* (New York, NY: St. Martin's Press, 2001), p. 80.

4. Christopher Anderson, "Madonna Rising: The Wild and Funky Early Years in New York," *New York*, October 14, 1991.

5. Morton, p. 92.

6. Bob Grossweiner and Jane Cohen, "Industry Profile: Camille Barbone," Celebrity Acess © 2001–2006 Gen-Den Corporation, http://www.celebrityaccess.com/news /profile.html?id=280.

7. "Madonna: She's One Lucky Star!," *Teen*,1984.

8. "Madonna and Child, The New Baby, The New Life," *Vanity Fair*, March 1998, http://www.fortunecity.com /tinpan/underworld/437/vf.htm.

9. Morton, p. 104.

10. Frank Owen, *Clubland: The Fabulous Rise and Murderous Fall of Club Culture* (New York, NY: St. Martin's Press, 2003).

11. "Mark Kamins: Legendary USA Disc Jockey," DJ Portal, September 20, 2003, http://djsportal.com/en/pioneer/ index.php?id=mark.

Chapter 5: Star Light, Star Bright

1. Pamela Robertson, "Guilty Pleasures," *Guilty Pleasures: Feminist Camp from Mae West to Madonna* (Durham, NC: Duke University Press, 1996), p. 123.

2. "MTV News; Madonna Raw—The Early Years," http:// www.fortunecity.com/tinpan/underworld/437/raw.htm.

3. Ibid.

4. Christopher Connelly, "Madonna Goes All the Way," *Rolling Stone*, November 22, 1984.

5. "MTV News; Madonna Raw—The Early Years," http:// www.fortunecity.com/tinpan/underworld/437/raw.htm.

6. Andrew Morton, *Madonna* (New York, NY: St. Martin's Press, 2001), p. 126.

7. Becky Johnston, "Confession of a Catholic School Girl," *Interview Magazine*, 1989.

8. Ibid.

Chapter 6: Why's It So Hard

1. Pamela Robertson, *Guilty Pleasures: Feminist Camp from Mae West to Madonna* (Durham, NC: Duke University Press, 1996), p. 127.

2. "MTV News; Madonna Raw—The Early Years," http://www.fortunecity.com/tinpan/underworld/437/raw.htm.

3. "Sean Penn—Madonna Would Have Ruined My Life," *Britain Now Magazine*, April 21, 2005, http://www.femalefirst.co.uk/celebrity/36042004.htm.

4. Michael Goldberg, "Performance Review: Madonna Seduces Seattle," *Rolling Stone*, May 23, 1985.

5. Becky Johnston, "Confession of a Catholic School Girl," *Interview*, 1989.

6. "Madonna's Road to Matrimony Wasn't Studded with Success," Sky News-London, January 24, 2001, http://www.foxnews.com/story/0,2933,606,00.html.

7. Andrew Morton, *Madonna* (New York, NY: St. Martin's Press, 2001), p. 138.

8. Bill Zehme, "Madonna," *Rolling Stone*, March 23, 1989.

9. "Sean Penn—Madonna Would Have Ruined My Life," *Britain Now*, April 21, 2005, http://www.femalefirst.co.uk/celebrity/36042004.htm.

10. Stephen Holden, "Madonna Goes Heavy on Heart," *New York Times*, June 29, 1986.

11. Greg Kot, "Without the videos, her albums just aren't the same," *Chicago Tribune*, May 13, 1990.

12. Robert Hilburn, "Madonna Is Nobody's Toy," *Los Angeles Times*, July 6, 1986.

13. Michael Gilmore, "The Madonna Mystique," *Rolling Stone*, September 10, 1987.

14. Ibid.

15. Morton, p. 143.

Chapter 7: I Can Feel Your Power

1. J. D. Considine, "Madonna's True Confessions," *Rolling Stone*, April 6, 1989.

2. "Music, Myth and Controversy," *Songtalk*.

3. Bill Zehme, "Madonna," *Rolling Stone*, March 23, 1989.

4. C. W. Arrington, "Madonna Is in Bloom: Circe at Loom," *Time*, May 20, 1991.

5. Any Cohen, "Madonna's Andy Cohen Interview: EW's guest editor questions the queen of pop." *Entertainment Weekly*, August 16, 2016, http://ew.com /article/2016/08/16/madonna-andy-cohen-ew-interview.

6. "Music, Myth and Controversy," *SongTalk*.

7. "Madonna and Child: The New Baby, the New Life," *Vanity Fair*, March 1998, http://www.fortunecity.com/tinpan /underworld/437/vf.htm#.

8. Camille Paglia, "Venus of the Radio Waves," *Sex, Art and American Culture* (New York, NY: Vintage Books, 1992), p. 11.

9. AbsoluteMadonna.com, "Blond Ambition Tour 1990," http://www.absolutemadonna.com/tours /ba.shtml.

10. Don Shewey, "Madonna: The Saint, the Slut, the Sensation," *Advocate*, 1991, http://www.donshewey.com /music_articles/madonna1.htm.

11. Alek Keshishian, *Truth or Dare*, Boy Toy Productions/ Miramax Films, 1991.

12. Shewey.

13. "Vanilla Ice," http://en.wikipedia.org/wiki/Vanilla_Ice.

14. bell hooks, "Madonna: Plantation Mistress or Soul Sister?" in *Black Looks: Race and Representation* (London, UK: Turnaround, 1992).

15. Douglas Crimp and Michael Warner, "No Sex in Sex" in Lisa Frank and Paul Smith, *Madonnarama: Essays on*

Sex and Popular Culture (San Francisco, CA: Cleis Press, 1993), p. 95.

16. Ibid.

17. Ibid.

18. Don Romesburg, "Madonna Dares," *Advocate*, May 11, 1999.

19. Peter Wilkinson, "Madonna's Favorite Filmmaker Is One Smart Alek," *Rolling Stone,* May 16, 1991.

20. Ibid.

21. "In Bed with Madonna/Truth or Dare film review," *New Internationalist*, August 1991, http://www.newint.org /issue222/reviews.htm.

22. Shewey.

23. Wilkinson.

Chapter 8: Never Forget Who You Are

1. Madonna, *Sex* (New York, NY: Warner Books, 1992).

2. Janet Maslin, "Dangerous Game," *New York Times*, 1993, http://movies2.nytimes.com/gst/movies/movie.html?v_ id=123054.

3. Angie Hung, "High Flying Adored: Madonna Tribe Meets Tim Rice," 2005, http://www.madonnatribe.com/idol /timrice.htm.

4. Mim Udovitch, "Madonna," *US Magazine*, January 1997

5. Ibid.

6. Andrew Morton, *Madonna* (New York, NY: St. Martin's Press, 2001), p. 213.

7. Larry King, "Madonna Reviews Life," *Larry King Live*, http://www.cnn.com/SHOWBIZ/Music/9901/19 /madonna.lkl.

8. Ingrid Sischy, "Madonna and Child: The New Baby, the New Life," *Vanity Fair*, 1998, http://www.fortunecity.com /tinpan/underworld/437/vf.htm.

9. Barry Walter, "Madonna Just Made Her Most Daring Album in Years," *Spin*, 1998, http://www.madonna-online.ch/m-online/interviews/interview-sites/98-04_spin-interview.htm.

10. Miranda Sawyer, "It's My Love You But F*** You Record," *Face*, 2000, http://www.madonnavillage.com/library/interviews/theface2000.html.

11. Ibid.

Chapter 9: This Guy Was Meant for Me

1. Andrew Morton, *Madonna* (New York, NY: St. Martin's Press, 2001), p. 231.

2. Jill Smolowe, Pete Norman, Joanne Fowler, Caris Davis, et al., "Kilt by Association."

3. Ibid.

4. Alex Needham, "Madonna: London Earl's Court," *NME*, 2001, http://www.madonna-online.ch/m-online/tours/01_dwt/reviews/dwt-reviews.htm.

5. "Crazy Jamie: Madonna Tribe Meets Jamie King," Madonna Tribe, 2005, http://www.madonnatribe.com/idol/jamie_one.htm.

6. "Crazy Jamie: Madonna Tribe Meets Jamie King."

7. Corey Moss, "Madonna Twirls Rifle, Lifts Up Her Kilt at Opener," MTV News Archive, May 25, 2004, http://www.mtv.com/news/articles/1487434/20040525/nullmadonna.html.

8. "A Madonna Discography, 2001–2006," http://www.matthewhunt.com/madonna/tours.html.

9. John Wiederhorn, "Madonna Yanks Controversial American Life Video," MTV.com, March 31, 2003, http://www.mtv.com/news/articles/1470876/20030331/madonna.jhtml?headlines=true.

10. "Material Girl Goes from Madonna to Esther: Singer Adopts Hebrew Name as a Way to Show Interest in Kabbalah," June 18, 2004, http://www.msnbc.msn.com/id/5234922.

11. Harry Smith, "Madonna: Diva, Author, Housewife," *The Early Show*, http://www.cbsnews.com/stories/2004/12/20/earlyshow/leisure/celebspot/main661931.shtml.

12. Karen Springen, "Writing Dynamo: Children's Author Jane Yolen has published nearly 300 books, but she's got plenty more stories to tell," August 12, 2005, http://www.msnbc.msn.com/id/8917828/site/newsweek.

13. Terri Gross, "Madonna: Pop Icon, Children's Writer," Fresh Air from WHYY, November 23, http://www.npr.org/templates/story/story.php?storyId=4183844&sourceCode=RSS.

14. "Entertainment Briefs," http://cbs2chicago.com/entertainmentbriefs/ARCHIVE/20051020/resources_entertainment_html.

15. Absolute Madonna website, http://www.absolutemadonna.com/tours/confessions.shtml.

16. "Madonna to Help Orphaned Children in Africa,"People.com, August 3, 2006, <http://people.aol.com/people/article/0,26334,1222452,00.html.

17. Ibid.

18. Ibid.

19. Ibid.

20. Raising Malawi, http://www.raisingmalawi.org/about-us-#about-us-2.

21. Joey Bartolomeo and Rennie Dyball, "Madonna & Guy Ritchie: How It Fell Apart," *People*, November 3, 2008, http://people.com/archive/cover-story-madonna-guy-ritchie-how-it-fell-apart-vol-70-no-18.

22. Natalie Clarke, "Why sad, haunted David Banda is the REAL victim of Madonna's divorce," *Daily Mail*, October 16, 2008, http://www.dailymail.co.uk/tvshowbiz/article-1078044/Why-sad-haunted-David-Banda-REAL-victim-Madonnas-divorce.html.

23. Barbara Jones, "Don't let Madonna adopt your twins! Family of Mercy, 10, warn girls' father: 'You'll never see

them again.'" *Daily Mail,* February 4, 2017, http://www
.dailymail.co.uk/news/article-4192028/Mercy-s-uncle
-tells-twins-family-not-let-Madonna-adopt.html.

24. Tom Sykes, "How Madonna Lost the Bitter Custody Battle
Over Son Rocco," Daily Beast, September 9, 2016, http://
www.thedailybeast.com/articles/2016/09/10/how
-madonna-lost-the-bitter-custody-battle-over-son-rocco
.html.

25. Gary Susman, "'Swept Away' sweeps anti-
Oscars." *Entertainment Weekly,* March 21, 2013, http://
ew.com/article/2003/03/21/swept-away-sweeps-anti
-oscars.

26. A. O. Scott, "FILM REVIEW; No Madonna Is an
Island." *New York Times*, October 11, 2002, http://www
.nytimes.com/movie/review?res=9D05E7DA173AF932A2
5753C1A9649C8B63.

27. Madonna's kids in the making of Swept Away. Directed by
Guy Ritchie. 2002. LourdesLeonOnline, 2011.

28. Charlotte Bailey, "Guy Ritchie brands marriage to
Madonna a 'circus.'" *Telegraph*, October 16, 2008, http://
www.telegraph.co.uk/news/celebritynews/3208229/Guy
-Ritchie-brands-marriage-to-Madonna-a-circus.html.

29. Esther Lee, "Madonna 'Felt Incarcerated' by Guy Ritchie
During Their Marriage." *Us Magazine*, March 11, 2015,
http://www.usmagazine.com/celebrity-news/news
/madonna-felt-incarcerated-by-guy-ritchie-during
-marriage-2015113.

30. Roxane Gay and Arianne Phillips. "Madonna's Spring
Awakening," *Harper's Bazaar*, January 10, 2017, http://
www.harpersbazaar.com/culture/features/a19761
/madonna-interview.

31. Joey Bartolomeo and Rennie Dyball, "Madonna & Guy
Ritchie: How It Fell Apart," *People*, November 3, 2008.

Chapter 10: Veni, Vidi, Vici

1. Ingrid Sischy. "Madonna: The one and only, on her life
unchained," Interview, CNET Networks, April 21, 2008.

2. Helen Brown, "Madonna: The mother of reinvention," *Telegraph*, August 25, 2008, http://www .telegraph.co.uk/culture/music/rockandjazzmusic/3559140 /Madonna-the-mother-of-reinvention.html.

3. Nigel Smith, "Madonna Tells a New York Crowd Why Her 'MDNA Tour' (Airing on Epix) Was the Hardest She'd Ever Done," IndieWire, June 19, 2013, http://www.indiewire .com/2013/06/madonna-tells-a-new-york-crowd-why-her -mdna-tour-airing-on-epix-was-the-hardest-shed-ever -done-37477.

4. Boy Toy, Inc., August 27, 2012, http://www.madonna.com /news/title/the-mdna-tour-in-madonnas-own-words.

5. Full Speech: Madonna introduces Pussy Riot, 2014, mymdna.com.

6. MDNA World Tour, DVD, Directed by Danny B. Tull and Stephanie Stennour, Universal Music Distribution, 2013.

7. Neil McCormick, "Madonna, Hyde Park, review, *Telegraph*, July 17, 2012, http://www.madonna.com/news/title/the -mdna-tour-in-madonnas-own-words.

8. Maura Johnston, "Madonna Has an Identity Crisis on MDNA," *Village Voice*, March 28, 2012, http://www .villagevoice.com/music/madonna-has-an-identity-crisis -on-mdna-6434430.

9. Randall Roberts, "In her element for the world to see," *L.A. Times*, February 6, 2012, http://articles.latimes .com/2012/feb/06/entertainment/la-et-madonna-super -bowl-20120206.

10. Alex von Tunzelmann, "W.E.'s a royal scandal! Madonna fails to read all about it," *Guardian*, January 26, 2012, https://www.theguardian.com/film/2012/jan/26/we-royal -scandal-madonna.

11. SABC News, February 3, 2012, http://www.sabc.co.za /news/a/4745b2004a0826b59bb0ffa3aed19366/Madonna -excited-about-Super-bowl-performance-20120203.

12. Joe Berkowitz, *Fast Company*, February 7, 2012, http:// www.webcitation.org/6KBbIUYMV.

13. Julia Kaganskiy, Creators.vice.com, February 6, 2012, https://creators.vice.com/en_us/article/meet-the-team -behind-the-projections-at-madonnas-super-bowl-2012 -halftime-show.

14. Berkowitz.

15. Jen Chaney, "Madonna and the Super Bowl halftime show: A play-by-play," *Washington Post,* February 5, 2012, https://www.washingtonpost.com/blogs/celebritology /post/madonna-and-the-super-bowl-halftime-show-a -play-by-play/2012/02/05/gIQAlJuisQ_blog.html?tid=a_ inl&utm_term=.de397588f1fd#pagebreak.

16. Ken Tucker, "Madonna at the Super Bowl review," *Entertainment Weekly*, February 5, 2012, http:// ew.com/article/2012/02/05/madonna-super-bowl-cee-lo -green-nicki-minaj-m-i-a-lmfao.

17. Jocelyn Vena, MTV News, February 6, 2012, http://www .mtv.com/news/1678574/madonna-super-bowl-halftime -show.

18. Gary Graff, "Madonna, prepping for tour, says she 'appreciates' her hometown." *Oakland Press*, July 17, 2015, http://www.theoaklandpress.com/article/OP/20150717 /ENTERTAINMENT/150719588.

19. John Bream, "Madonna more playful than provocative in Xcel show," *Star Tribune,* October 9, 2015, http://www .startribune.com/review-madonna-more-playful-than -provocative-in-sold-out-show/331504611/#1.

20. Joe Lynch, "Madonna Gets Surprisingly Nostalgic at First NYC Tour Stop, Then Kicks Amy Schumer's Ass," *Billboard*, September 17, 2015, http://www.billboard .com/articles/review/6699797/madonna-rebel-heart-nyc -tour-amy-schumer-madison-square-garden.

21. Brian Hiatt, "Madonna on Making 'Rebel Heart,' the Age of Distraction and Joan of Arc," *Rolling Stone*, March 15, 2015, http://www.rollingstone.com/music/features /madonna-on-making-rebel-heart-the-age-of-distraction -and-joan-of-arc-20150305.

22. Ibid.

23. Josh Duboff, "2016 Met Gala Best Dressed Celebrities," *Vanity Fair,* May 2016, http://www.vanityfair.com/style /photos/2016/05/met-gala-best-dressed-red-carpet-2016.

24. "Where's the rest of the material, girl? Flesh-flashing Madonna, Lady Gaga and Katy Perry lead the staggeringly-bad worst dressed brigade at the Met Gala" Read more: http://www.dailymail.co.uk/femail/." Daily Mail, May 2, 2016 http://www.dailymail.co.uk/femail/ article-3570313/A-red-carpet-catastrophe-Selena-Gomez- suffers-rare-fashion-fail-leads-host-staggeringly-bad- sartorial-slip-ups-year-s-star-studded-Met-Gala.html.

25. Julie Miller, "Madonna Claims Her Risqué Met Gala Outfit Was 'a Political Statement,'" *Vanity Fair,* March 4, 2016, http://www.vanityfair.com/style/2016/05/madonna -met-gala-outfit.

26. Emma Spedding,"Met Gala 2016: Madonna's Givenchy look is inspired by 'kinesiology tape'," *Telegraph*, May 3, 2016, http://www.telegraph.co.uk/fashion/events /met-gala-2016-madonnas-givenchy-look-is-inspired-by -kinesiology.

27. Evan Real, "Madonna Defends Met Gala 2016 Outfit to 'Ageist' Critics: It Was a 'Political Statement'," *Us Magazine,* May 5, 2016, http://www.usmagazine.com/celebrity-news /news/madonna-my-met-gala-2016-outfit-was-a-political -statement-w205344.

Conclusion

1. Madonna's Full Acceptance Speech at Billboad Women in Music 2016, Video, *Billboard*, 2016, http://www.billboard .com/video/madonnas-full-acceptance-speech-at -billboard-women-in-music-2016-7624369.

2. Joe Lynch, "Madonna Delivers Her Blunt Truth During Fiery, Teary Billboard Women In Music Speech," *Billboard*, December 9, 2016, http://www.billboard.com /articles/events/women-in-music/7616927/madonna -billboard-woman-of-the-year-labrinth.

3. Ibid.

4. Ibid.

5. Ibid.

6. Full Speech: Madonna introduces Pussy Riot, 2014, mymdna.

7. Ibid.

8. Madonna's Full Acceptance Speech at Billboard Women in Music 2016.

GLOSSARY

Alvin Ailey American Dance Theater A renowned dance conservatory in New York City that is known for training some of the best dancers in the world.

Boy Toy A man who is valued for the pleasure he gives a woman; arm candy or a trophy husband/boyfriend.

disco A type of dance music that features elements of funk and soul; it was popular during the 1970s and early 1980s.

Eva "Evita" Perón The second wife of Argentine President Juan Perón, Evita is famous for her compassion for Argentina's working-class citizens—and for being played by Madonna in the 1996 film adaptation of her life.

feminism The idea that women should be treated equally to men, including receiving equal opportunities, equal pay, and equal rights under the law.

gold record When an album (or single) reaches 500,000 sales units.

Kabbalah An ancient Jewish translation of the Bible.

Madonna In Biblical reference, Madonna is Mary, the mother of Jesus. A "Madonna" is also a term for a very beautiful and virtuous woman.

Malawi A small, poorly developed country in Africa, Malawi has been nicknamed "The Warm Heart of Africa."

Material Girl A counterpart to the Boy Toy, a Material Girl is a woman who values things over people or experiences and wants only the finest luxuries.

MTV Launched in 1981, MTV (Music Television) is the first television channel dedicated to music and music videos.

objectify To degrade. Usually used to explain how women are treated when they are made into sex symbols and treated as objects of desire and not as intelligent, worthwhile people.

platinum record When an album (or single) reaches one million sales units.

pop music Music that is very current and of-the-moment; something you hear on the radio and that has mass appeal.

single A song that is released to radio to promote an album. Before MP3s, singles were the only songs you could hear without having to buy the full album.

Studio 54 The most famous disco club in the world, Studio 54 was known for attracting celebrities—and drugs.

FURTHER READING

Books

Morgan, Michelle. *The Mammoth Book of Madonna.* Philadelphia, PA: Running Press, 2015.

Sullivan, Caroline. *Madonna: Ambition. Music. Style.* London, UK: Carlton Books, 2015.

Websites

Madonna

www.madonna.com

The official Madonna website, it includes information about the artist as well as upcoming tour dates and album releases.

Madonnalicious

www.madonnalicious.com

A fan site dedicated to Madonna, this website features news and biographical information about the artist.

Film

Goldthorpe, Maureen. *Madonna: Goddess of Pop.* Phase4 Films, 2013.

Madonna Celebration: The Video Collection. WarnerBros, 2009.

INDEX

J

Jackson, Michael, 10, 12, 28, 41, 56

"Joan of Arc," 97, 98

K

Kabbalah, 74, 85

Kamins, Mark, 39

Keshishian, Alek, 66

King, Jamie, 79

King, Martin Luther, Jr., 9

L

Lambert, Mary, 43, 50

Lang, Pearl, 31–33, 74, 83

Leon, Carlos, 46, 72–73, 80

Leon, Lourdes Maria Ciccone (daughter), 12, 15, 23, 49, 73, 74, 76–79, 87

Leonard, Pat, 46

Let Me Tell You a Secret, 83

Like a Prayer, 46, 56, 57

"Like a Prayer," 59, 61, 95

"Like a Virgin," 10, 44, 93

lingerie, 15, 39, 62

Live-Aid, 49

"Lucky Star," 41

M

Madonna, 41

Malawi, 84–85, 87

"Masterpiece," 93, 94

"Material Girl," 48, 50

Material Girl (fashion brand), 23

Maverick Entertainment, 23, 68–69

Max's Kansas City, 36

Mazar, Debi, 63

MDNA, 93

MDNA tour, 23, 91, 94, 95

"Mer Girl," 20

Michigan, University of, 26, 30

"Miles Away," 89

Minaj, Nicki, 16

"Mother and Father," 20

MTV, 10–12, 15, 43–44, 48, 85

Music, 77, 78, 80

N

New Music Seminar, 43

Ninja, Luis, 63

O

Oates, John, 43

Obama, Barack, 9

Orbit, William, 73–75, 93

P

"Papa Don't Preach," 50, 56

paparazzi, 51–52, 72

Parker, Alan, 71

Patterson, Vincent, 61

V

Y